TOUGH AS STEEL

PITTSBURGH STEELERS
2006 Super Bowl Champions

SP
SPORTS PUBLISHING
L.L.C.

SportsPublishingLLC.com

PITTSBURGH TRIBUNE-REVIEW™
TRIBUNE-REVIEW™
TRIB TOTAL MEDIA

SportsPublishingLLC.com

PITTSBURGH TRIBUNE-REVIEW™
TRIBUNE-REVIEW™
TRIB TOTAL MEDIA

Joseph J. Bannon Sr. and Peter L. Bannon publishers

Susan M. Moyer senior managing editor

Noah Adams Amstadter acquisitions editor

Travis W. Moran developmental editor

K. Jeffrey Higgerson art director

Joseph Brumleve cover design, imaging

Kenneth J. O'Brien interior layout

Heidi Norsen interior layout, imaging

Erin Linden-Levy photo editor

Richard M. Scaife Publisher Inc. publisher

Ralph J. Martin president/ceo

Frank L. Craig editor

Robert Fryer managing editor

James J. Cuddy Jr. senior deputy managing editor

Richard A. Monti senior deputy managing editor

James M. Kubus deputy managing editor, design

Kevin Smith executive sports editor

Mike Orfanopoulos deputy sports editor

ISBN (Hardcover): 1-59670-074-2   ISBN (Softcover): 1-59670-083-1
Front cover photo by Chaz Palla/Trib Total Media
Back cover photo by Philip G. Pavely/Trib Total Media
Printed in the United States of America
Sports Publishing L.L.C. 804 North Neil Street • Champaign, IL 61820 • Phone: 1-877-424-2665 • Fax: 217-363-2073
SportsPublishingLLC.com

CONTENTS

PRESIDENT'S NOTE

Let me begin by joining the rest of the Steelers Nation in congratulating the Pittsburgh Steelers on their fifth Super Bowl Championship. It's been a long time coming, but we finally got our "one for the thumb!"

The city that gave birth to the Steel Curtain in the 1970s has undergone dramatic changes since our last Super Bowl victory. The steel mills that lined our three rivers are mostly gone, replaced by world-class health care and technology industries.

But many of our traditions remain.

That blue-collar work ethic and devotion to the Steelers made famous three decades ago thrives today. The Terrible Towels created by Myron Cope in the 1970s still wave by the thousands each Sunday. We still break out into Steelers chants (Here we go Steelers ... here we go!) at most public gatherings, and even after the season ends, Steelers jerseys remain in our wardrobe rotation. No matter where Pittsburgh natives eventually land, they never lose their passion for the team that's given them so much to cheer for over the years.

Our heartfelt congratulations go out to the Rooney family, Coach Bill Cowher, and the entire team on their accomplishments this season. To Jerome Bettis, we say thanks for so many years and so many great plays. We hope this wasn't our last Bus ride, but we wish you all the best.

It's been our pleasure to provide our readers with comprehensive coverage of the Steelers this season. We're looking forward to bringing you more great coverage in the future.

Sincerely,

Ralph J. Martin

Ralph J. Martin
President & CEO
Tribune-Review Publishing Co.
Trib Total Media

FOREWORD

MYRON COPE
RETIRED — JUNE 2005

Author of Double Yoi!, *available in updated soft cover in June 2006.*

You could have fooled me. In fact, the Super Bowl XL Pittsburgh Steelers indeed fooled me, giving me the sense that over 35 years spent broadcasting Steelers games as a radio color analyst, I had not learned very much about football.

Through late November into early December, when the Steelers floundered through a three-game losing streak, I gave up on them. Forget the playoffs, I figured. Somehow, at that point, they came together as a force and convincingly won their requisite final four regular-season games. By then any fool could see they were special, as I at last saw from my place in the crowded compound for dimwits. Bottom-seeded for the playoffs and thus facing three road games to make the Super Bowl, their unprecedented accomplishment reminded me of a time—way back in the Great Depression—when my dad often took me to Pittsburgh Pirates baseball games at old Forbes Field. "Stay here and stay out of trouble," he would say, placing me in a general-admission seat. He then took a place among the gamblers who always stood behind the third-base seats and called out bets on just about every possibility—for example, even the next pitch, ball or strike?

The Pirates trailed, 10-0, and a guy yelled, "One hundred to one the Pirates lose." My dad answered, "I'll take a dollar!" He won a hundred bucks—big money then—and we ate steak.

Did the Steelers ever eat steak! They rode a seven-game streak into the Super Bowl, beating opponents by an average of 17 points. As we well know, The Bus—Jerome Bettis—made, and emphatically earned, his storybook return to his hometown, Detroit, for the Big One. Through it all, as he executed his specialist's assignment to move the pile, he reminded me of an aging New York Giants running back who thundered his way to victory over Buffalo in Super Bowl XXV.

"Do you remember Ottis Anderson?" I asked the Bus a few years ago.

"Oh, certainly," he replied.

The Bus played the sport hard, appreciated its history, and treated it with respect by never failing to show up on game day dressed in a sharp, freshly pressed business suit with tastefully matching necktie. It was time for business.

The pages that follow will vividly recall the chapters that unfolded in a Steelers season that only can be characterized in terms of greatness. These awakened memories will serve the football fan well, especially those fans worldwide who make up the Steelers Nation. All nations require a flag, of course. Thus, the Steelers Nation's flag—The Terrible Towel—now flies as never before, from Iraq and Afghanistan to New Mexico and Nova Scotia.

Question: When was the last time the Dallas Cowboys were called "America's Team"?

Legendary Steelers broadcaster Myron Cope speaks to the crowd during a halftime ceremony honoring his 35 years with the team.
Philip G. Pavely/Trib Total Media

PARKER, BIG BEN LEAD STEELERS

BY JOE BENDEL

A soft-baking sun hovered above Heinz Field for what turned out to be an ideal day for football. The thermometer hit 75 degrees at kickoff, the clouds gave way to riveting blue skies, and quarterback Ben Roethlisberger reached perfection.

Literally.

Roethlisberger quashed all those preseason concerns about the offense—not to mention the potential for his own Sophomore Jinx—by producing a perfect passer rating in leading the Steelers to a season-opening, 34-7, victory over the Tennessee Titans.

He also remained perfect as a regular-season starter, pushing his career record to 14-0.

The 2004 Rookie of the Year was stunningly efficient yesterday, going 9 of 11 for 218 yards with two touchdowns in a game that took just 2 hours and 35 minutes. He is the first quarterback since Trent Green of the Chiefs in 2003 to amass a perfect rating of 158.3.

Roethlisberger's rating in the preseason was 32.8.

"When you only throw a couple balls, it's not hard to (have a perfect rating)," said Roethlisberger, whose 11 attempts were the fewest by a Steelers quarterback since Terry Bradshaw attempted nine against Cincinnati on October 17, 1977. "You get the ball close to our receivers, and they're going to make plays. They did it today."

Second-year tailback Willie Parker mirrored his quarterback and nearly hit perfection as well, blasting through and blowing by the Titans for 161 yards on 22 carries (7.3 per attempt), including an 11-yard touchdown. He also took a screen pass 48 yards for a total of 209 yards from scrimmage.

In just his second career start, Parker produced the best opening-day effort in Steelers history—surpassing Frenchy Fuqua's 114 yards in 1971—and the 12th-best single-game rushing effort.

And to think, Parker entered training camp as the Steelers' fourth-team tailback behind Jerome Bettis, Duce Staley and Verron Haynes. Bettis (calf) and Staley (knee) missed the game with injuries, and they could find themselves behind Parker on the depth chart when they return.

Coach Bill Cowher was asked if Parker, who ran for 102 yards in the regular-season finale at Buffalo last season, would start next week in Houston.

"There's a good chance," Cowher said. "He ran very well. I see no reason to make a change at this point."

As far as Roethlisberger is concerned, Cowher was comforted in seeing his young quarterback erase the question marks that surrounded him coming into the season.

Eluding Tennessee's Rocky Boiman (50) and picking up extra yardage is Pittsburgh running back Willie Parker.
Christopher Horner/Trib Total Media

"There's been a lot of criticism thrown at him, but he's never really wavered at all," Cowher said. "He's a very confident young man. I don't think he was bothered by the things that were said and the concerns that a lot of people had, myself included. He'd say, 'Just relax, coach, we'll be OK.' (I said), 'OK, well show me.' He got a good start today."

The Steelers, coming off a 15-1 season that ended in the AFC title game, came out sluggish on defense.

The Titans, using a three tight-end set, easily moved 61 yards in 11 plays behind the passing of quarterback Steve McNair (4 for 5) and the running of Chris Brown (24 yards). Tight end Ben Troupe ended the drive with a 1-yard touchdown reception.

But that's as good as it would get for the Titans, as the Steelers performed a methodical version of the Tennessee Waltz from there.

The Steelers' Antwaan Randle El catches a touchdown pass over his shoulder in front of Tennessee's Tank Williams during the second quarter.
Christopher Horner/Trib Total Media

They scored on their first six possessions, including four in the first half, and did not turn the ball over. Tennessee, which went 5-11 last season, turned it over four times, two leading to scores.

On the Steelers' first drive, Roethlisberger went 5 for 5 for 88 yards, with the final pass going to rookie tight end Heath Miller. The highlight was a screen pass to Parker, who followed blocks by linemen Kendall Simmons, Marvel Smith and Alan Faneca, along with wideout Hines Ward, for a 48-yard gain to the Tennessee 4.

"I think we caught them with their pants down," Parker said of the perfectly timed play. "They weren't looking forward to that."

Kicker Jeff Reed sandwiched two first-half field goals—the first coming after linebacker James Farrior forced a fumble, the second on an interception by safety Troy Polamalu—around a 63-yard touchdown reception by wideout Antwaan Randle El, who gave the Steelers a 17-7 lead with 8:49 left before halftime.

The Steelers padded their lead to 27-7 on the opening drive of the second half, on the strength of a 26-yard catch by Randle El, a 14-yarder by wideout Cedrick Wilson and an 11-yard scoring run by Parker that saw him bounce off of two Tennessee defenders en route to the end zone.

Haynes provided the final points with a 5-yard scoring run, which was set up by a 45-yard burst by Parker that prompted the crowd to begin a chant of "W-I-L-L-I-E! ... W-I-L-L-I-E."

"It felt great to see the fans backing me," Parker said, sporting a wide smile at the end of a perfect day for football at Heinz Field.

	1st	2nd	3rd	4th	Final
Titans	7	0	0	0	7
Steelers	7	13	14	0	34

SCORING SUMMARY

1st

TEN B. Troupe 1-yard pass from S. McNair (R. Bironas kick)—11 plays, 61 yards in 6:37.

PIT H. Miller 3-yard pass from B. Roethlisberger (J. Reed kick)—9 plays, 77 yards in 5:41.

2nd

PIT J. Reed 44-yard FG—7 plays, 14 yards in 3:16.

PIT A. Randle-El 63-yard pass from B. Roethlisberger (J. Reed kick)—1 play, 63 yards in 0:10.

PIT J. Reed 27-yard FG—10 plays, 80 yards in 5:32.

3rd

PIT W. Parker 11-yard run (J. Reed kick)—6 plays, 74 yards in 3:23.

PIT V. Haynes 5-yard run (J. Reed kick)—9 plays, 80 yards in 4:59.

4th

No scoring.

TEAM STATS

	TITANS	STEELERS
1st Downs	16	18
3rd-Down Conversions	3-8	5-11
4th-Down Conversions	0-0	0-0
Punts-Average	2-46.0	3-45.7
Punts-Returns	1-10	1-0
Kickoffs-Returns	6-132	2-40
Int.-Returns	0-0	2-20
Penalties-Yards	7-49	3-27
Fumbles-Lost	4-2	0-0
Time Of Pos.	29:10	30:50
Total Net Yards	303	424
Total Plays	53	52
Net Yards Rushing	97	206
Rushes	23	41
Net Yards Passing	206	218
Comp.-Att.	18-27-2	9-11-0
Yards Per Pass	11.5	3.2
Sacked-Yards Lost	0-0	3-13
Red Zone Efficiency	1-3-33%	3-4-75%

NEARLY PERFECT DOMINANCE

BY JOE BENDEL

Good thing they opened the roof at Reliant Stadium. Otherwise, the Steelers might have blown the thing right off.

As it was, the Steelers delivered a Texas-sized thrashing in the sweltering heat, one in which they unleashed their battering ram defense (eight sacks), their hot-handed quarterback (another near-perfect performance) and their fleet-footed running back (111 yards) in a 27-7 victory.

And, for anyone who thought the Steelers might have been looking ahead to next weekend's AFC championship-game rematch with the Patriots at Heinz Field, forget about it.

Their focus was squarely on a Texans team (0-2) that wilted while safety Troy Polamalu amassed three sacks, quarterback Ben Roethlisberger went 14 of 21 for 254 yards with two touchdowns (139.8 passer rating) and tailback Willie Parker topped the 100-yard mark for the second consecutive week with 111 on 25 carries with a score.

Before the Texans could come up for air, the score was 20-0 at the half, and, the Steelers were well on the way to their second victory without a loss.

Now, they can focus on that showdown with Super Bowl champion New England, which lost to Carolina yesterday.

"This is what we expect," left tackle Marvel Smith said, referring to the Steelers' near-flawless execution, including no turnovers for the second consecutive week. "If we go out and take care of the ball, run the ball and play physical, we should pretty much be able to dominate every Sunday. It's just a matter of focusing on the game at hand. We weren't thinking about the Patriots. We weren't thinking about anything but winning another game."

When will Smith and Co. start thinking about the Patriots?

"I'm not worried about them right now," he said. "We'll take this one, enjoy it, then move on to the next."

There were possibilities that yesterday's game could have been a trap for the Steelers, considering Houston is a struggling team and the Steelers have some business to take care of next with the Patriots. But safety Chris Hope firmly stated that there was no chance of that happening.

"Our coaching staff wouldn't let us," he said. "Yeah, you could get caught up in the big game with New England. But we approach every team the same way, whether they're 0-12 or the defending Super Bowl champion. You can't afford to let down in this league, otherwise, you won't accomplish what we've set out to accomplish."

Pittsburgh's Troy Polamalu drops Houston Texans quarterback David Carr for a third-quarter sack at Reliant Stadium. Polamalu had three sacks on the day. *Philip G. Pavely/Trib Total Media*

What the Steelers accomplished yesterday was another efficient effort on both sides of the ball—they defeated Tennessee, 34-7, a week earlier—and a ringing endorsement for Roethlisberger, Parker and a

defense, led by Polamalu, that's allowed just 14 points and registered 10 sacks in two games.

"I said this before, and I even told the team last night: Until we show an ability to do things

Steelers quarterback Ben Roethlisberger celebrates a third-quarter touchdown pass to Willie Parker. Roethlisberger threw for 254 yards and two touchdowns against Houston. *Philip G. Pavely/Trib Total Media*

consistently, 'Who are we?'" Coach Bill Cowher said. "I think you have to do that for the first month of the season, start doing some things consistently. You have to develop the right habits and the right expectations. We're playing smart, we're not turning the football over, we have minimal penalties (five for minus-40 yards yesterday). Those are the things that showed up these two weeks, but we have a big test next week. I think they lost today, and they're going to come in with a chip on their shoulder."

The Steelers wasted little time setting the tone yesterday. Parker, who had 161 yards a week earlier, ran for 19 yards on the game's first play. He and Roethlisberger, who was listed as questionable with a knee injury, combined for 60 yards on that opening series, with Parker producing 39. The Steelers took a 3-0 lead on a 37-yard field goal by Jeff Reed, who broke Gary Anderson's team record for consecutive field goals with 20.

Then came the bumbling Texans offense, which turned the ball over five times a week earlier. They didn't disappoint, losing the ball on their first possession when linebacker Clark Haggans forced embattled quarterback David Carr into a fumble that was recovered by linebacker Joey Porter at the Texans' 22.

The Steelers needed just two plays, a six-yard run by Parker and a 16-yard touchdown reception by Hines Ward, for a 7-0 lead.

Next came a nine-play, 92-yard drive by the Steelers in which Roethlisberger went 5 of 6 for 98 yards (two Steelers penalties added yardage to the drive). The final play was a 14-yard touchdown pass to Ward and a 17-0 lead. Reed added another field goal before the half.

Houston cut the margin to 20-7 to open the third, but just when the momentum appeared to be shifting, Roethlisberger closed the door. On third-and-five from the Steelers 37, he was trapped, but slid to his right, pumped and threw deep across the field to wide receiver Cedrick Wilson, who caught the ball 40 yards downfield. Three plays later, Parker sealed the win with a 10-yard touchdown run.

"I made some plays early, Ben followed me up, then the defense stopped them pretty much all game," Parker said. "I'd say that's a pretty good formula. You can't really lay it out better than that. We have to keep it that way, now, keep playing that kind of football. Because we have a real tough one ahead of us."

	1st	2nd	3rd	4th	Final
Steelers	10	10	7	0	27
Texans	0	0	7	0	7

SCORING SUMMARY

1st

PIT   J. Reed 37-yard FG—11 plays, 61 yards in 4:53.

PIT   H. Ward 16-yard pass from B. Roethlisberger (J. Reed kick)—2 plays, 22 yards in 0:35.

2nd

PIT   H. Ward 14-yard pass from B. Roethlisberger (J. Reed kick)—9 plays, 92 yards in 4:21.

PIT   J. Reed 35-yard FG—8 plays, 69 yards in 4:20.

3rd

TEX   D. Davis 3-yard pass from D. Carr (K. Brown kick)—14 plays, 78 yards in 7:55.

PIT   W. Parker 10-yard run (J. Reed kick)—6 plays, 68 yards in 3:14.

4th
No Scoring.

TEAM STATS

	STEELERS	TEXANS
1st Downs	18	16
3rd-Down Conversions	4-11	8-15
4th-Down Conversions	1-2	0-1
Punts-Average	1-39.0	4-40.2
Punts-Returns	2-10	1-6
Kickoffs-Returns	1-19	5-101
Int.-Returns	0-0	0-0
Penalties-Yards	5-40	7-58
Fumbles-Lost	0-0	1-1
Time Of Pos.	29:06	30:54
Total Net Yards	388	221
Total Plays	54	59
Net Yards Rushing	135	113
Rushes	32	25
Net Yards Passing	253	108
Comp.-Att.	14-21-0	16-26-0
Yards Per Pass	11.5	3.2
Sacked-Yards Lost	1-1	8-59
Red Zone Efficiency	3-5-60%	1-1-100%

BRADY, PATS TRUMP STEELERS

BY JOE BENDEL

Moments after Hines Ward enlivened the Heinz Field crowd with a game-tying touchdown reception, he stuck his head underneath a towel.

"I didn't even want to watch," said the Pro Bowl wideout, whose four-yard score with 1:21 remaining evened things at 20-20 against the defending Super Bowl Champion New England Patriots. "I couldn't watch."

Ward's greatest fear soon came to fruition—and the towel proved to be of absolutely no help. Patriots quarterback Tom Brady calmly walked onto the field and engineered a magical and methodical drive that ended with a 43-yard field goal by Adam Vinatieri with a second remaining.

And just like that, the Steelers were on the wrong end of a 23-20 outcome—compliments of the coolest quarterback in the game.

"He's the best in the business. He's the reason they've won three of four championships," Ward said. "They had a great (kickoff) return before that last series, and I was just hoping our defense would hold up, maybe get a turnover. Maybe the Patriots would make a mistake. But, hey, they didn't do it. They played a full 60 minutes. We played 59. They're the champions."

Brady was 12 of 12 for 168 yards in the fourth quarter and 3 of 3 for 37 yards on that final drive. He assumed control at the Patriots 38, following a 34-yard kickoff return by Ellis Hobbs, and quickly hit running backs Kevin Faulk and Patrick Pass with underneath passes of 17 and 14 yards. He deftly attacked the Steelers linebacking corps on both plays, noting that his backs had golden opportunities to find open spots in the Steelers' zone.

"That's what a good quarterback does," said Steelers cornerback Deshea Townsend, who watched Brady finish 31 of 41 for 372 yards with no touchdowns, an interception and three sacks. "He takes what you give him."

Brady completed one more pass on that final drive—a six-yarder to David Givens after a Steelers timeout—and Vinatieri did the rest. It was Brady's fourth victory in five games against the Steelers, including AFC Championship wins in 2001 and 2004 at Heinz Field. He improved his career mark to 59-15 as a starter.

The Steelers watched their 16-game regular-season winning streak get snapped, and quarterback Ben Roethlisberger had his NFL-record 15 consecutive regular-season victories as a starter broken. A year earlier, the Steelers snapped New England's NFL-record 18-game winning streak at Heinz Field.

Steelers receiver Hines Ward catches a touchdown pass well above his New England defenders. *Christopher Horner/Trib Total Media*

The Patriots (2-1), though, made amends by beating the Steelers in the AFC title game.

"If I can predict the future, maybe we can switch what happened last year," linebacker Larry Foote said. "They win the first one, we win the second. That would be best. We just have to put this behind us right now and move on."

The teams went toe-to-toe much of the game, with Patriots running back Corey Dillon (22 carries for 61 yards) scoring from 4 yards out to open the scoring, and the Steelers tying it on an 85-yard touchdown reception by Ward. Jeff Reed added a 33-yard field goal to give the Steelers a 10-7 lead, which they took into the half.

Reed added a second field goal in the third quarter for a 13-7 edge, but the Patriots, who lost by 10 to Carolina last week, sandwiched a seven-yard touchdown run by Dillon between two Vinatieri field goals to make it 20-13 with 3:19 remaining.

The going is rough for Steelers running back Willie Parker as New England's Ty Warren applies pressure during the first half.
Christopher Horner/Trib Total Media

Roethlisberger, who was sacked four times and finished 12 of 28 for 216 yards with two touchdowns, ran an efficient late-game drive before facing a fourth-and-11 at the Patriots 27. He threw a fade to Quincy Morgan down the left sideline and Morgan drew an interference call on former Steelers cornerback Chad Scott at the 4. Ward scored on the next play, beating Scott.

But Brady was up to the task again, though it wasn't all him. The Patriots defense held Steelers star running back Willie Parker, who entered with 272 yards and a 5.8 average, to 55 yards on 17 carries for a 3.2 average. They also threw a variety of defensive looks at Roethlisberger—who admitted to being uncertain at times—and were beneficiaries of some untimely gaffes and penalties by the Steelers.

Two will stand out the most: Wide receiver Antwaan Randle El's decision to pitch the ball back to Ward after a 49-yard catch that was fumbled and recovered by New England at its own 11 ("It cost us at least a field goal," Ward said.); and an illegal procedure call against tackle Barrett Brooks that nullified a successful 47-yard field goal by Reed, who then missed from 52 yards out with 2:37 left in the first half.

In the previous two weeks, the Steelers thumped Tennessee and Houston by a combined 61-14, but they saw this game as their true test. They'll have to regroup after failing to run the ball effectively, allowing four sacks (two by Richard Seymour), not making the Patriots pay for 10 penalties and three turnovers and not making stops at the end of the game after loosening up on defense.

"I'm not going to walk around and sulk," Ward said. "It's a game, you learn from it, and you come back. Maybe we'll see them again."

	1st	2nd	3rd	4th	Final
Patriots	7	0	3	13	23
Steelers	10	0	3	7	20

SCORING SUMMARY

1st

NE — C. Dillon 4-yard run (A. Vinatieri kick)—7 plays, 46 yards in 3:33.

PIT — H. Ward 85-yard pass from B. Roethlisberger (J. Reed kick)—1 play, 85 yards in 0:15.

PIT — J. Reed 33-yard FG—7 plays, 34 yards in 2:57.

2nd

No Scoring.

3rd

PIT — J. Reed 24-yard FG—6 plays, 22 yards in 2:56.

NE — A. Vinatieri 48-yard FG—4 plays, 0 yards in 0:51.

4th

NE — C. Dillon 7-yard run (A. Vinatieri kick)—7 plays, 86 yards in 3:42.

PIT — A. Vinatieri 35-yard FG—7 plays, 59 yards in 4:08.

PIT — H. Ward 4-yard pass from B. Roethlisberger (J. Reed kick)—9 plays, 51 yards in 1:58.

NE — A. Vinatieri 43-yard FG—5 plays, 37 yards in 1:20.

TEAM STATS

	PATRIOTS	STEELERS
1st Downs	24	14
3rd-Down Conversions	8-16	3-13
4th-Down Conversions	0-0	0-0
Punts-Average	4-45.0	6-44.2
Punts-Returns	4-55	3-20
Kickoffs-Returns	5-128	4-79
Int.-Returns	0-0	1-5
Penalties-Yards	10-118	5-35
Fumbles-Lost	3-2	1-1
Time Of Pos.	35:23	24:37
Total Net Yards	426	269
Total Plays	74	55
Net Yards Rushing	80	79
Rushes	30	23
Net Yards Passing	346	190
Comp.-Att.	31-41-1	12-28-0
Yards Per Pass	7.9	5.9
Sacked-Yards Lost	3-26	4-26
Red Zone Efficiency	2-5-40%	1-3-33%

IN THE KICK OF TIME

BY JOE BENDEL

This was one of those made-for-TV slugfests, a game that featured more counterpunches than a heavyweight boxing match.

A record crowd at Qualcomm Stadium hung on every catch, every run, every big hit—many waving white Chargers towels; others waving Terrible Towels—as the Steelers and San Diego staged the Game of the Year on Monday Night Football.

The end result: Steelers 24, Chargers 22.

The winning points came on a 40-yard field goal by Steelers kicker Jeff Reed with 6 seconds left, following a 50-yard drive by the Steelers.

And although that last drive led to the win, it could have proven costly. Quarterback Ben Roethlisberger's knee buckled after a hit by the Chargers' Luis Castillo and he was helped off the field after laying motionless with 1:05 remaining. Backup Charlie Batch handed the ball off three times to Jerome Bettis before Reed's kick.

Roethlisberger's status was not immediately known after the game. His injury comes on the heels of a calf injury to No. 2 quarterback Tommy Maddox, who was de-activated for the game.

Coach Bill Cowher could not elaborate on Roethlisberger's condition.

"It looked bad from what I saw up on the screen," Cowher said. "But I don't have (an update) right now."

Roethlisberger was seen on crutches after the game and in noticeable pain.

Batch said he's ready if Roethlisberger is out for an extended period.

"This is why you work hard at all times; you never know when you'll be needed," Batch said.

The Steelers held a 14-7 lead at the half, but the Chargers chipped away at the lead. Three field goals by Nate Kaeding put San Diego up, 16-14, with 11:41 remaining. The Steelers, who struggled moving the ball in the third quarter, needed just three Roethlisberger passes—33 and 13 yards to Hines Ward and 16 to tight end Heath Miller—to take a 21-16 lead. Miller blew by Chargers linebacker Shawne Merriman for his second career touchdown catch with 10:30 remaining.

The Chargers did not flinch. Tomlinson, who was held to less than 100 yards for the first time in two weeks, scored from 2 yards out with 4:42 remaining to give the Chargers a 22-21 lead. He was stopped on a 2-point conversion run.

That set up the late-game heroics for the Steelers (3-1).

The Chargers (2-3) entered with one of the league's most potent offenses, having scored 86 points the previous two games, but the Steelers stifled them early. San Diego managed just one first down in the

Jeff Reed's 40-yard field goal with six seconds left gave the Steelers a victory over San Diego, 24-22. *Chaz Palla/Trib Total Media*

first quarter, failed to cross the 50 and looked nothing like the team that had defeated the Giants and Patriots in Weeks 3 and 4.

The dangerous triumvirate of running back LaDainian Tomlinson, tight end Antonio Gates and quarterback Drew Brees combined for just 21 yards.

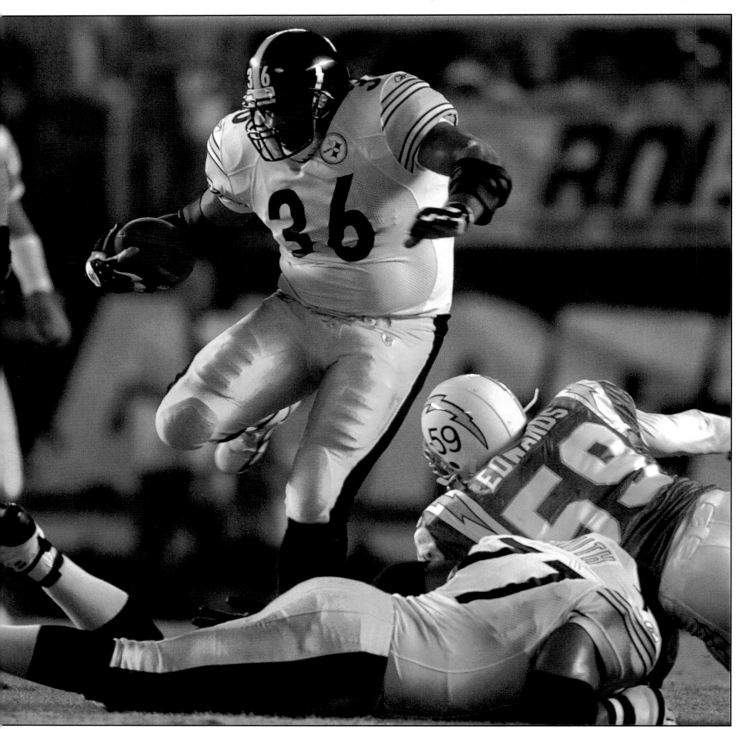

Jerome Bettis hurdles teammate Marvel Smith as he looks for extra yards against the Chargers. *Chaz Palla/Trib Total Media*

The Steelers, though, were nearly as ineffective in the opening quarter, failing to muster a first down in their first two possessions, then turning it over on a fumble by quarterback Ben Roethlisberger after taking a hit from Chargers linebacker Shawne Merriman.

But the flow of the game shifted in the second quarter, as the offenses became rejuvenated. The Steelers appeared to be reinvigorated by the return of tailback Jerome Bettis, who'd missed the previous three games with a calf injury. He ripped off a 16-yard gain on a screen pass in the first quarter, sending a message he was back to full health, then reeled off runs of 5, 3, 2 and 5 yards in helping the Steelers score the game's first touchdown on the opening possession of the second quarter.

The Steelers thought they had scored on the sixth play of that possession, when Hines Ward made a diving catch, got up, and zigzagged his way to the end zone for what appeared to be a 47-yard touchdown. But the Chargers challenged and Ward was ruled down by contact at the Chargers 33.

The Steelers were undaunted by the reversal. Roethlisberger hit wideout Antwaan Randle El for a 21-yard gain, Bettis ran for 5 yards, then Roethlisberger ran in from 7 yards out. Roethlisberger, lined up in the shotgun, masterfully ran a quarterback draw, following his blockers and barreling into the end zone. He spiked the ball after the score, looking into a crowd that was chock-full of Steelers fans.

The Chargers answered by moving the ball to the Steelers 35 on the ensuing possession—a 15-yard catch by Gates, his first—was the highlight, but linebacker James Harrison ended the drive in highlight-reel fashion. Starting for the injured Clark Haggans, Harrison retrieved a pass that hit off the hands of Gates, by tipping the ball to himself and pulling it in. He wasn't done there. He sprinted ahead, then hurdled Tomlinson. The airborne Harrison found a way to keep his balance after his circus move and set the Steelers up at the Chargers 41.

Eight plays later—after runs of 14 yards by Willie Parker, eight by Roethlisberger and six by Bettis—the Steelers made it 14-0 when Bettis leapt through a

crease on the left side of the line with 1:37 remaining in the second quarter.

The Chargers answered quickly. Brees completed passes of 15 and 23 yards before finding Gates on a slant pattern from 11 yards out to make it 14-7 with 34 seconds remaining. The Steelers went into intermission with the seven-point advantage.

	1st	2nd	3rd	4th	Final
Steelers	0	14	0	10	24
Chargers	0	7	6	9	22

SCORING SUMMARY

1st
No scoring.

2nd
PIT   B. Roethlisberger 7-yard run (J. Reed kick)—9 plays, 84 yards in 5:33.
PIT   J. Bettis 1-yard run (J. Reed kick)—7 plays, 41 yards in 2:56.
SD   A. Gates 11-yard pass from D. Brees (N. Kaeding kick)—4 plays, 47 yards in 1:03.

3rd
SD   N. Kaeding 34-yard FG—7 plays, 47 yards in 2:13.
SD   N. Kaeding 32-yard FG—8 plays, 45 yards in 2:53.

4th
SD   N. Kaeding 41-yard FG—6 plays, 62 yards in 3:50.
PIT   H. Miller 16-yard pass from B. Roethlisberger (J. Reed kick)—3 plays, 62 yards in 1:11.
SD   L. Tomlinson 2-yard run (run failed)—11 plays, 62 yards in 5:48.
PIT   J. Reed 40-yard FG—11 plays, 40 yards in **4:36.**

TEAM STATS

	STEELERS	CHARGERS
1st Downs	25	20
3rd-Down Conversions	4-10	5-12
4th-Down Conversions	0-0	0-0
Punts-Average	6-42.7	4-48.2
Punts-Returns	1-0	2-11
Kickoffs-Returns	6-138	5-157
Int.-Returns	1-25	0-0
Penalties-Yards	11-104	9-100
Fumbles-Lost	1-1	1-1
Time Of Pos.	33:23	26:37
Total Net Yards	311	279
Total Plays	61	57
Net Yards Rushing	104	66
Rushes	32	21
Net Yards Passing	207	213
Comp.-Att.	17-26-0	20-35-1
Sacked-Yards Lost	3-18	1-6
Red Zone Efficiency	3-3-100%	2-4-50%

BACKUP PLAN FAILS

BY JOE BENDEL

Jacksonville linebacker Mike Peterson recounted his brief conversation with injured Steelers quarterback Ben Roethlisberger, moments after the Jaguars posted a 23-17 overtime win at blustery Heinz Field.

"He said it wouldn't have ended up like it did if he was out there," said Peterson, one of three Jaguars players to intercept Roethlisberger's replacement, Tommy Maddox, on Sunday. "I just turned to him and said, 'I don't know about that.' We came here ready to play our style of football."

Or, as Jaguars defensive end Marcellus Wiley said, "We weren't coming in here backing down against them because they're the Steelers and they were in the AFC Championship game last year. That doesn't mean anything to us. What matters is what we did to them today.

"This is 2005. It was 1 o'clock on Sunday. We came out and said, 'What are you going to do?' We thrive when teams think they're going to out-bully us. You saw what we did out there. Nobody in the NFL is going to out-physical us. The Steelers couldn't do it today."

The Steelers' problems went beyond physically matching up with a Jaguars team (4-2) that won the game on a 41-yard interception return in overtime by cornerback Rashean Mathis, who sniffed out a curl pattern to Steelers wideout Quincy Morgan and went untouched to the end zone.

Maddox, who hadn't started a meaningful game since Week 2 of last season, played like the anti-Roethlisberger, throwing the three picks (Roethlisberger's thrown none), amassing a passer rating of 30.1 (Roethlisberger's rating is a league-best 123.8) and failing to win in his first start of the season (Roethlisberger is 16-1 as a regular-season starter).

"Rusty," Wiley said, in describing Maddox. "We could see it."

And the Jaguars pounced, consistently tipping passes at the line of scrimmage and sacking Maddox twice. Also, Maddox's four turnovers (three interceptions, one fumble) tripled the Steelers' season total, from two to six.

"You want to get that backup a little flustered," said Peterson, who acknowledged that the Jaguars prepared all week as if Roethlisberger was going to start, despite a hyperextended/bruised left knee. "I'd say he probably got rattled."

It didn't help matters that Maddox was without his top pass-catcher in wideout Hines Ward, who missed his first career game with a hamstring injury. Ward, though, might not have been able to help Maddox, particularly during that forgettable overtime period.

Steelers backup quarterback Tommy Maddox (8) fumbles the snap during overtime, as Jacksonville's Reggie Hayward (97) closes in and recovers the ball. *Christopher Horner/Trib Total Media*

Maddox had a chance to salvage a miserable day after Morgan returned the overtime kickoff 74 yards to the Jaguars 26. That alone might have been enough for kicker Jeff Reed to win the game, but two plays after tailback Willie Parker (55 yards on 21 carries) nearly lost a fumble, Maddox did Parker one better and lost the ball on third-and-11 from the Jaguars 27.

Maddox planned a pitch to Parker, but mishandled the snap, ran into fullback Dan Kreider,

then kicked the loose ball backward, leading to a recovery by the Jaguars' Reggie Hayward.

The play quashed any hope of Reed attempting a 44-yard kick. Reed missed from 46 yards out with 3:28 remaining in regulation.

"We just blundered it," center Jeff Hartings said of the first overtime possession.

"We didn't focus," said All-Pro guard Alan Faneca, who not only saw the Steelers (3-2) lose their second

Steelers tight end Heath Miller brushes off Jacksonville defender Deon Grant for a second-quarter touchdown at Heinz Field. Despite the 15-yard touchdown, the Steelers dropped the game, 23-17, in overtime. *Philip G. Pavely/Trib Total Media*

consecutive home game, but also fall 1 1/2 games behind AFC North leader and next week's opponent Cincinnati (5-1). "I reminded everybody before we went out there that we had to focus, but we lost our concentration—and you saw the result."

While those in the Jaguars locker room were celebrating, the mood was decidedly different for a Steelers team that was coming off a short week and playing without its top two offensive players. Tailback Jerome Bettis, who ran the ball 17 times last Monday night, carried just four times for 4 yards yesterday.

"I was a spectator out there," Bettis said tersely, after being asked about Jacksonville's ability to jump on the Steelers' pass routes. "I can't give you much more than that."

Was he upset about being a "spectator?"

"Very upset," he said, before taking a pause. "I'm upset we lost, not about being a spectator. That's my role."

Bettis mostly watched as the Steelers managed just 73 rushing yards on 30 carries, held the ball for 27:27 and went 1 of 12 (8 percent) on third-down conversions. Maddox finished 11 of 28 for 154 yards with a touchdown and the three interceptions. A bright spot on offense was tight end Heath Miller, who had a team-high four catches for 72 yards with a 27-yarder and a 15-yard touchdown.

The Jaguars, who finished with 246 total yards, trailed 14-10 at the half. The Steelers first-half scores came on a Miller catch and a 72-yard punt return by Antwaan Randle El, while the Jags scored on a 7-yard run by Greg Jones (after a Maddox pick) and a 23-yard field goal. The Jags went ahead 17-14 on a 10-yard catch by Matt Jones before Reed hit a 29-yard field goal with 9:38 remaining that sent the game into overtime.

	1st	2nd	3rd	4th	OT	Final
Jaguars	7	3	7	0	6	23
Steelers	0	14	0	3	0	17

SCORING SUMMARY

1st

JAX   G. Jones 7-yard run (J. Scobee kick)—1 play, 7 yards in 0:07.

2nd

PIT   H. Miller 15-yard pass from T. Maddox (J.Reed kick)—4 plays, 65 yards in 1:20.

PIT   A. Randle El 72-yard punt return (J. Reed kick).

JAX   J. Scobee 23-yard FG—6 plays, 10 yards in 1:43.

3rd

JAX   M. Jones 10-yard pass from B. Leftwich (J.Scobee kick)—6 plays, 71 yards in 3:14.

4th

PIT   J. Reed 29-yard FG—11 plays, 69 yards in 5:14.

OT

JAX   R. Mathis 41-yard interception return.

TEAM STATS

	JAGUARS	STEELERS
1st Downs	17	16
3rd-Down Conversions	7-19	1-12
4th-Down Conversions	0-1	0-0
Punts-Average	9-46.9	6-31.7
Punts-Returns	3-15	5-94
Kickoffs-Returns	2-40	2-77
Int.-Returns	3-54	1-0
Penalties-Yards	10-106	7-80
Fumbles-Lost	1-0	2-1
Time Of Pos.	34:06	25:54
Total Net Yards	246	218
Total Plays	73	60
Net Yards Rushing	93	73
Rushes	35	30
Net Yards Passing	153	145
Comp.-Att.-Int.	19-35-1	11-28-3
Sacked-Yards Lost	3-24	2-9
Red Zone Efficiency	2-3-66%	1-2-50%

36 JEROME BETTIS

There's no way it could end this way.

Jerome Bettis couldn't end his storied career as the Steelers' power running back with a goal-line fumble late in a do-or-die playoff game against the Indianapolis Colts.

Would his career end without making it to his hometown of Detroit to play in the Super Bowl?

Fate smiled on him in Indianapolis, as the Steelers held on for a 21-18 victory in their AFC divisional playoff game.

And again the next week in the AFC title game at Denver.

"I can't imagine anything better," Bettis said after the 34-17 win over the Denver Broncos clinched the Steelers' Super Bowl berth. "I'm going home."

And his teammates wanted nothing more than to take The Bus to Detroit—and get him a Super Bowl ring.

Wide receiver Hines Ward cried openly last year after losing to the New England Patriots, saying that the team, fearing Bettis would not return for another season, couldn't bring him to the Super Bowl.

Bettis, the fifth all-time rusher in NFL history (13,662 yards), delayed retirement for one more season—a lucky 13th as it turned out—for the chance to play in Super Bowl XL at Ford Field.

"What better way to go than to go the place where it all started for him," Ward said. "But we don't want to be content with just getting him there. We want him to win."

Bettis came to the Steelers before the 1996 season after spending his first three years with the Los Angeles/St. Louis Rams. Following a disappointing 1995 season, where he rushed for just 637 yards, Bettis re-established himself as one of the premier running backs in the NFL in his first season in Pittsburgh by running for 1,431 yards and 11 TDs.

Bettis would go on to rush for over 1,000 yards in his first six seasons with the Steelers. And though he hasn't hit that mark since the 2001 season, he's still a big contributor to the Steelers' offense. The last two seasons alone have seen him rush for 22 of his career 91 TDs.

Will the Super Bowl be Bettis' final game?

"That's a great question," Bettis said. "I'm going to look at it. The last thing I want to do is diminish anything by even thinking about that. This is a great opportunity we have. I'm going to wait until after the Super Bowl and think about it."

Over the years, Bettis has been dogged by knee problems, asthma and other assorted injuries, but the fans have never strayed. They religiously packed into the taping of his weekly "Jerome Bettis Show" and, during what was likely his last game at Heinz Field on New Year's Day against the Detroit Lions, begged him to stay with chants of "One More Year!"

"I've got so much respect for Jerome and what he's brought to this football team," said Steelers coach Bill Cowher. "My relationship with him is he's a classy guy, and he's been such an inspiration."

Bettis showed his leadership skills on the eve of the AFC Championship game in Denver when he spoke up during a team meeting. He delivered an impassioned pep talk, imploring his Steelers teammates to complete two tasks.

"Give 110 percent," Bettis said. "And get me home."

Bettis had been 0-3 in AFC Championship games since joining the Steelers in 1996. Last year, he was stopped early on a fourth-and-1 and was stuffed twice

within the five-yard line late in what turned out to be a 41-27 loss to the New England Patriots.

It was near the end of that game that Steelers quarterback Ben Roethlisberger made a promise to Bettis.

"I was in the middle of tears," Bettis recalled. "We were on the sidelines, the clock was winding down, and it was obvious we had lost the game. He was boohoo-ing; I was boohoo-ing. He turned to me and said, 'Come back. I'll get you to the Super Bowl. Just come back. Give me one more year.' "

Roethlisberger didn't let Bettis down.

—Jim Rodenbush

STEELERS POUND UPSTART BENGALS

BY JOE BENDEL

Chad Johnson went into his flashy dance routine way too early. The Bengals wideout had just completed an end zone cha-cha-cha when his apparent touchdown got overturned because he was out of bounds.

"He's down there doing his thing, thinking to himself, 'I scored!'" Steelers linebacker Joey Porter said. "The place is going crazy, people are fired up."

Then …

"Silence," Porter said.

The Bengals got nothing out of that opening-game possession—kicker Shayne Graham missed a 30-yard field goal—and the momentum swung faster than a Pittsburgh-built wrecking ball. The missed opportunity was a harbinger of things to come for a Bengals team that still can't beat the Steelers, evidenced by a 27-13 loss in front of a record crowd at Paul Brown Stadium.

"We had it on the bulletin board all week—'This is our division,'" Steelers linebacker Larry Foote said. "We're on top, and we plan to stay there."

Actually, the Steelers (4-2) are a half-game behind the Bengals (5-2), but yesterday's game went a long way in proving that power still overrides finesse in the AFC North. And, it didn't hurt to have starting quarterback Ben Roethlisberger (two touchdown passes) and wideout Hines Ward back in the lineup, a week after both missed an overtime loss to Jacksonville due to injury.

"We did it our way, by running the ball and playing strong defense," said Ward, who had three catches for 35 yards with a touchdown, including a Riverdance celebration mimicking his friend Johnson. "It's the Steeler way."

Perhaps the Bengals would have had their way, had they not managed just three points on the first two possessions. They traveled to the Steelers 12 to open the game and to the Steelers 8 on their second possession.

"But they only get a field goal. That was critical," said Steelers tailback Jerome Bettis, who punished the Bengals with 56 yards on 13 carries. "Three points after all of that?"

Once the Bengals made it clear they couldn't throw the knockout punch, the Steelers bullied them the rest of the game. They ran the ball better than they have all season (Willie Parker had 131 of the Steelers' 221 rushing yards), they dominated in time of possession (35:29 to 24:31) and their defense made quarterback Carson Palmer (53.8 passer rating) and Johnson (who was stymied by shadowing cornerback Ike Taylor) look ordinary.

It was a standard recipe for the Steelers, who averaged 158 yards rushing in their two victories over Cincinnati last season.

Steelers teammates Ben Roethlisberger and Jeff Hartings celebrate a third-quarter touchdown against the Bengals at Paul Brown Stadium. The score put the Steelers up 17-6 as they went on to defeat the Bengals 27-13. *Philip G. Pavely/Trib Total Media*

"We came in here and played our kind of football, kind of forced our will on them a little bit," Pro Bowl guard Alan Faneca said.

The Steelers won a franchise-record 10th consecutive road game and dispatched the Bengals for the sixth time in seven games. The defense held the Bengals' second-ranked offense to nearly 13 points below its average and forced two turnovers against a team that rarely gives the ball away.

The Steelers took a 7-6 lead into the half before laying into the Bengals in the final two quarters. A skittish Palmer, unable to take advantage of Ben Roethlisberger's first interception of the year, threw a pair of picks on the Bengals' first two possessions of the second half, one by Steelers safety Chris Hope that led to a field goal and another by defensive end Aaron Smith that led to a score and a 17-6 Steelers lead.

Palmer had gone 20 quarters and 169 pass attempts without throwing an interception before his meltdown in the third quarter.

"What we did was take the running game away," said Foote, mindful the Steelers allowed just 91 rushing yards. "That caused problems everywhere else."

The Steelers running game caused its own set of problems for the Bengals. Parker, who'd been limited to 81 yards the previous two games, ripped off a 37-yard touchdown run to make it 17-6 with 7:48 left in the third quarter. After that, he and Bettis took turns torturing the Bengals, who owned the ball for only 13-plus minutes over the final three quarters. The Steelers held the ball for 21 minutes, 58 seconds in the second half.

The defense of the Steelers—Troy Polamalu, Larry Foote (50), and Aaron Smith (91)—delivers a blow to Cincinnati's Chris Perry in the second quarter. *Philip G. Pavely/Trib Total Media*

The Steelers did not attempt a pass in the fourth quarter (Roethlisberger threw for only 93 yards), running the ball 19 times.

"This is what we do," Bettis said. "And until you stop it, we're going to keep doing it."

	1st	2nd	3rd	4th	Final
Steelers	0	7	17	3	27
Bengals	3	3	0	7	13

SCORING SUMMARY

1st
CIN   S. Graham 26-yard FG—11 plays, 69 yards in 4:56.

2nd
PIT   H. Miller 2-yard pass from B. Roethlisberger (J. Reed kick)—9 plays, 60 yards in 5:22.
CIN   S. Graham 39-yard FG—9 plays, 72 yards in 3:30.

3rd
PIT   J. Reed 27-yard FG—4 plays, 6 yards in 2:04.
PIT   W. Parker 37-yard run (J. Reed kick)—3 plays, 47 yards in 1:12.
PIT   H. Ward 4-yard pass from B. Roethlisberger (J. Reed kick)—10 plays, 60 yards in 6:16.

4th
PIT   J. Reed 39-yard FG—10 plays, 49 yards in 6:18.
CIN   C. Palmer 4-yard run (S. Graham kick)—7 plays, 79 yards in 0:55.

TEAM STATS

	STEELERS	BENGALS
1st Downs	20	20
3rd-Down Conversions	4-11	3-11
4th-Down Conversions	0-0	0-0
Punts-Average	2-38.5	4-37.5
Punts-Returns	3-20	1--6
Kickoffs-Returns	2-31	6-115
Int.-Returns	2-55	1-0
Penalties-Yards	5-65	4-35
Fumbles-Lost	1-1	0-0
Time Of Pos.	35:29	24:31
Total Net Yards	304	302
Total Plays	62	57
Net Yards Rushing	221	91
Rushes	47	19
Net Yards Passing	83	211
Comp.-Att.-Int.	9-14-1	21-36-2
Sacked-Yards Lost	1-10	2-16
Red Zone Efficiency	2-4-50%	1-3-33%

The Bengals' Rudi Johnson gets wrapped up by Pittsburgh defenders Chris Hope (28), Willie Williams, and Troy Polamalu early in the game. *Philip G. Pavely/Trib Total Media*

"We had it on the bulletin board all week—'This is our division.' We're on top, and we plan to stay there."

—LINEBACKER LARRY FOOTE

STEELERS ESCAPE WITH LATE FIELD GOAL

BY JOE BENDEL

The Baltimore Ravens dressed up like a competent football team and put a scare into the Steelers at Heinz Field.

They entered as AFC North bottom-feeders and without star defenders Ray Lewis and Ed Reed, but came disguised as the Ravens of old and wreaked havoc for much longer than the crowd of 64,178 people had anticipated.

In the end, the Steelers squeaked by with a 20-19 victory, a margin that was far closer than the pregame double-digit point spread had indicated.

By kickoff, the Steelers were 14-point favorites.

By game's end, they were happy to escape with any type of win, considering it boosted their record to 5-2 and kept them a half-game behind the AFC North-leading Cincinnati Bengals (6-2). The Ravens dropped to 2-5 and 3-1/2 games out of first place.

Steelers kicker Jeff Reed hit a 37-yard field goal with 1:36 remaining for his second game-winning kick of the season, both occurring on Monday nights. He also beat the San Diego Chargers in Week 4.

The final scoring drive featured back-to-back completions of 14 and 23 yards by quarterback Ben Roethlisberger to Antwaan Randle El and Quincy Morgan to get things started. Verron Haynes followed with a 7-yard run on a draw, then tailback Jerome Bettis did the rest, carrying four consecutive times for 16 yards to set up Reed's winning kick.

The fired-up crowd was relieved, but only briefly. That's because the Ravens took over at their 31 with 1:29 remaining and drove to the Steelers 50 with less than a minute to play. But on third-and-three, Ravens quarterback Anthony Wright was thrown for a 3-yard loss by backup Steelers defensive end Brett Keisel.

"He had running room," Keisel said. "If I hadn't got to him there, he could have taken off."

Keisel's stop made it fourth-and-six from the Ravens' 47. Then, on the final play of the possession, Ravens running back Chester Taylor dropped a pass at the 50, ending Baltimore's hope of an upset in front of a national television audience.

"We knew this was going to be a battle," said Roethlisberger, who finished 18 of 30 for 177 yards with two touchdowns and two interceptions. "The fans and (the media) are the ones (who thought otherwise)."

For the Steelers, the victory not only ended an uncharacteristic two-game losing streak at Heinz Field, but also showcased rookie tight end Heath Miller, who scored both of the Steelers touchdowns and continued to emerge as a bona fide candidate for rookie of the year.

Steelers kicker Jeff Reed nails a 36-yard field goal to beat the Baltimore Ravens. *Chaz Palla/Trib Total Media*

The No. 1 draft choice gave the Steelers a 7-0 lead on the game's first possession with a 4-yard scoring reception, then scored on an 8-yard pass to open the third quarter, pushing the advantage to 17-10.

Miller had seven catches for 38 yards, bumping his totals to 21 for 204 with five touchdowns the past three games. He was wide open in the end zone on both of his touchdowns last night.

"They were good calls by Coach Whisenhunt," Miller said of offensive coordinator Ken Whisenhunt.

The Steelers nearly self-destructed midway through the fourth quarter. On fourth-and-10 from their 45, they botched a snap on a punt attempt. Up-

The Steelers' Hines Ward catches a tipped pass in front of Baltimore's Chad Williams (49) and Chris McAlister.
Christopher Horner/Trib Total Media

man Sean Morey walked up behind long snapper Greg Warren to warn his teammates that the Ravens had two returners back, including the dangerous Deion Sanders, but Warren snapped early and the ball hit Morey's leg.

Morey picked up the loose ball, then threw back to punter Chris Gardocki, who threw incomplete to Morey.

The Ravens took over at the Steelers 45 and turned the miscue into the go-ahead field goal, a 47-yarder by Matt Stover, who was 4 of 5 on the night. The Steelers then responded with the game-winning drive.

Heinz Field was filled with Terrible Towels, a tribute to retired color commentator Myron Cope, and the Steelers used that energy to jump on the Ravens. They went 79 yards in 15 plays to open the game, with the final 4 yards coming on the touchdown grab by Miller, who reversed his motion at the line of scrimmage and found a spot in the end zone.

Roethlisberger, who aggravated a right knee injury that he initially suffered in Week 1, completed seven of eight pass attempts on the opening drive, finding wide receiver Hines Ward four times for 48 yards. The drive lasted 8 minutes, 57 seconds, and the Steelers appeared to be picking up where they left off a week earlier in a 27-13 pounding of the Bengals.

It stood to reason that the Steelers had a chance of putting the game away at that early juncture, given the Ravens were the lowest-scoring team in the NFL (an average of 11.5 points per game) and their offense was being managed by Wright, a career backup.

But the Ravens' offense hardly looked anemic on the ensuing possession. The passing of Wright (4 of 6 on that drive) and the running of beleaguered back Jamal Lewis (3 carries for 22 yards) carried the Ravens to the Steelers 13 before Wright hit running Taylor for a 13-yard touchdown and a 7-7 tie.

A 42-yard field goal by Reed pushed the Steelers ahead, 10-7, early in the second quarter, thanks to a forced fumble by Steelers cornerback Deshea Townsend on the previous possession.

The Ravens also added a field goal, a 22-yarder by Stover, to head into halftime tied at 10-10.

After Miller's second touchdown, Stover connected on three field goals to put the Ravens ahead, 19-17, with 3:21 remaining. From there, Roethlisberger, Bettis and Reed put the finishing touches on the win, keeping the Steelers from getting tricked on Halloween night.

	1st	2nd	3rd	4th	Final
Ravens	7	3	0	9	19
Steelers	7	3	7	3	20

SCORING SUMMARY

1st
PIT   H. Miller 4-yard pass from B. Roethlisberger (J. Reed kick)—15 plays, 79 yards in 8:57.
BAL   C. Taylor 13-yard pass from A. Wright (M. Stover kick)—9 plays, 73 yards in 4:09.

2nd
PIT   J. Reed 42-yard FG—4 plays, 12 yards in 1:23.
BAL   M. Stover 22-yard FG—9 plays, 38 yards in 4:08.

3rd
PIT   H. Miller 8-yard pass from B. Roethlisberger (J. Reed kick)—10 plays, 64 yard in 5:55.

4th
BAL   M. Stover 40-yard FG—17 plays, 63 yards in 8:51.
BAL   M. Stover 49-yard FG—8 plays, 39 yards in 4:07.
BAL   M. Stover 47-yard FG—6 plays, 17 yards in 2:27.
PIT   J. Reed 37-yard FG—8 plays, 60 yards in 1:45.

TEAM STATS

	RAVENS	STEELERS
1st Downs	20	19
3rd-Down Conversions	9-18	4-12
4th-Down Conversions	1-3	1-2
Punts-Average	1-41.0	3-40.7
Punts-Returns	1-10	0-0
Kickoffs-Returns	4-75	5-127
Int.-Returns	1-28	2-0
Penalties-Yards	6-38	4-19
Fumbles-Lost	1-1	2-1
Time Of Pos.	31:04	28:56
Total Net Yards	318	261
Total Plays	73	61
Net Yards Rushing	72	101
Rushes	27	28
Net Yards Passing	246	160
Comp.-Att.-Int.	25-44-2	18-31-1
Sacked-Yards Lost	2-6	2-17
Red Zone Efficiency	0-0-0%	0-0-0%

RESERVES EXCEL

BY JOE BENDEL

Their No. 1 quarterback did not make the trip. Their MVP linebacker was out with a knee injury. And their starting tailback was hobbled by an ankle sprain.

The recipe for disaster? Almost.

But the Steelers dug deep into their depth chart, brushing the rust off running back Duce Staley, quarterback Charlie Batch and linebacker Clint Kriewaldt to win with all the beauty of a Sumo match.

They ultimately escaped storied Lambeau Field with a 20-10 victory against an error-prone Green Bay Packers team that slipped to 1-7.

"It wasn't pretty football, I know," said coach Bill Cowher, whose Steelers improved to 6-2 and remained a half-game behind first-place Cincinnati (7-2) in the AFC North. "But we made enough plays to win the football game and that's the bottom line."

Buoyed by an opportunistic defense (Troy Polamalu returned a fumble for a touchdown and Tyrone Carter intercepted a pass that set up another), Batch survived his first start in nearly four years. The Homestead native was summoned to replace the injured Ben Roethlisberger and passed for just 65 yards, which included a rating of 39.8 on 9-of-16 passing. He threw one interception and was held without a touchdown pass.

"We left a lot of plays on the field," said wideout Hines Ward, who had just one catch for 12 yards and is three receptions shy of John Stallworth's all-time franchise record. "But we won the game, and that's all that matters."

Batch had the good fortune of handing the ball off to the rejuvenated Staley, who had not run the ball since the AFC title game on January 23, 2004, and had played just once this season. The veteran back stepped in for the injured Willie Parker (who left early in the third quarter with an ankle sprain) and Jerome Bettis (who was de-activated due to a quadriceps strain) and produced 76 yards and a touchdown on 15 carries.

Staley's 3-yard score, on an off-tackle play that saw him shed would-be tackler Nick Barnett, turned a 13-10 lead into a 20-10 advantage with 6:16 remaining. It came four plays after Carter's interception of a pass by Brett Favre, who went 20 of 35 for 214 yards and was held without a touchdown pass at Lambeau Field for the first time in 28 games.

Staley celebrated his first touchdown since Oct. 10, 2004 by short-stepping his way into the end zone. It was a long time coming for a highly paid back who's sat silently while Parker and Bettis have owned the spotlight all season.

Steelers backup quarterback Charlie Batch escapes from Green Bay defender Kabeer Gbaja-Biamila during the third quarter at Lambeau Field.
Philip G. Pavely/Trib Total Media

Closing in on a fumble from Green Bay running back ReShard Lee are Troy Polamalu (43) and Chris Hope (28). Polamalu had two fumble recoveries on the day, including one for a touchdown, to lead the Steelers to a 20-10 victory. *Philip G. Pavely/Trib Total Media*

Staley entered training camp atop the depth chart, but had arthroscopic knee surgery for a torn lateral meniscus on August 8 and has been in the background ever since.

"It felt good to be out there with the guys, out there being able to contribute again," said Staley, who broke off a 17-yard run with 2:38 remaining that enabled the Steelers to run out the clock. "Coming into this game, I just said, 'Take what they give you. Don't turn the ball over and don't make mistakes.' I was truly blessed."

Added Pro Bowl guard Alan Faneca, "What we got out of Duce was huge. It was great to see him out there, getting after it and picking up huge chunks of yardage. Any time you see a guy who's been (sitting) down like that and waiting their turn, it's a good feeling to see him take advantage when the opportunity is there."

The way the first half went, it was anybody's guess as to when or if the Steelers would get to unveil Staley. Their offense stood and watched while the Packers mounted drives of 9 and 18 plays and held the ball for 18 minutes, 39 seconds, including 11:35 in the second period alone. Still, the Steelers had a 13-3 at the half, on the strength of Polamalu's 77-yard fumble return, set up by cornerback Bryant McFadden's hit on Favre.

Staley, meantime, had just 8 yards on three carries at the intermission. But, he assumed his thoroughbred form in the second half, which was crucial for a Steelers team that lost star linebacker James Farrior (knee) on the first series of the third quarter.

"I wanted to help us make some plays in the offense, control the ball," Staley said. "Coach had confidence in me."

Staley took over for Parker (13 yards on five attempts) on the second series of the third quarter and left little doubt that he'll be a viable option for the Steelers in the season's final months. He broke off runs of 17, 13, 9, 9, 7 and 6 yards during the stretch, the most important being the 3-yard score to seal the win.

"I knew we had to get the touchdown there to close it out," Staley said. "Just glad I was able to make it happen."

	1st	2nd	3rd	4th	Final
Steelers	6	7	0	7	20
Packers	3	0	7	0	10

SCORING SUMMARY

1st
PIT   J. Reed 32-yard FG—7 plays, 60 yards in 3:20.
PIT   J. Reed 24-yard FG—6 plays, 37 yards in 3:36.
GB   R. Longwell 40-yard FG—9 plays, 55 yards in 5:45.

2nd
PIT   T. Polamalu 77-yard fumble return (J. Reed kick)

3rd
GB   S. Gado 1-yard run (R. Longwell kick)—12 plays, 65 yards in 7:34.

4th
PIT   D. Staley 3-yard run (J. Reed kick)—4 plays, 20 yards in 1:55.

TEAM STATS

	STEELERS	PACKERS
1st Downs	13	16
3rd-Down Conversions	0-8	8-17
4th-Down Conversions	0-0	0-2
Punts-Average	4-45.8	3-49.0
Punts-Returns	3-13	4-66
Kickoffs-Returns	3-59	5-81
Int.-Returns	1-3	1-24
Penalties-Yards	4-53	8-74
Fumbles-Lost	3-0	3-2
Time Of Pos.	26:52	33:08
Total Net Yards	213	268
Total Plays	50	65
Net Yards Rushing	154	65
Rushes	33	29
Net Yards Passing	59	203
Comp.-Att.-Int.	9-16-1	20-35-1
Yards Per Pass	3.5	5.6
Sacked-Yards Lost	1-6	1-11
Red Zone Efficiency	1-3-33%	1-3-33%

"It wasn't pretty football, I know. But we made enough plays to win the football game and that's the bottom line."

—COACH BILL COWHER

STEELERS TOP BROWNS, LOSE BATCH

BY JOE BENDEL

The Steelers won a football game at Heinz Field, but lost another quarterback in the process.

Charlie Batch, who was replacing the injured Ben Roethlisberger for the second consecutive game, left with a fractured bone in his right pinkie finger late in the first half, giving way to third-teamer Tommy Maddox. Batch did not return for the Steelers' eventual 34-21 victory against the Cleveland Browns.

His status for next week was not immediately known, though coach Bill Cowher said it would likely be "a couple weeks" before Batch would return. The injury was described as a fractured metacarpal bone to the pinkie in his throwing hand.

Batch sustained the injury when his hand smashed into the helmet of a Cleveland Browns defender on a 15-yard completion to Hines Ward. The play gave Ward the Steelers all-time receptions record at 538, surpassing Hall of Famer John Stallworth.

Batch left the game after scoring on a 1-yard run with six seconds remaining before halftime. He said he could no longer bear the pain of taking snaps.

Batch finished 13 of 19 for 150 yards with a passer rating of 92.0.

"When you're going bone on helmet, you're not normally going to win," said Batch, who was then asked about his status for next week. "It all depends on the pain tolerance. We won't know that until we see if the swelling goes down the next couple of days."

Roethlisberger, who had arthroscopic surgery to repair a torn lateral meniscus November 3, could potentially be back next Sunday at Baltimore after missing the past two games. Hours after Roethlisberger's surgery, Cowher said it was "very conceivable" that Roethlisberger would be ready for the Ravens game.

Roethlisberger intensified his rehabilitation last week, saying he was ahead of schedule in strengthening the knee. Asked if he'd play next week moments after last night's game, Roethlisberger was cautiously optimistic.

"I don't know yet, we got a little urgency now, so we'll see," he said.

Despite the precarious nature of the Steelers quarterback position, they had little difficulty dispatching a Browns team that had no answer for record-breaking receiver Hines Ward (8 catches for 124 yards with a score), the trickery of the Steelers offense (wideout Antwaan Randle El hit Ward for a 51-yard touchdown), the first half play of Batch and an opportunistic Steelers defense that set up a touchdown and a field goal.

The Steelers improved to 7-2 and moved into a first-place tie in the AFC North Division with the

Steelers running back Jerome Bettis makes a move around the Cleveland defense during the second quarter. *Philip G. Pavely/Trib Total Media*

Cincinnati Bengals, who were idle yesterday. Second-place Cleveland fell to 3-6, four games behind the frontrunners.

The Browns looked like they might present a challenge early, as they drove 66 yards in 10 plays for a 7-0 lead on the opening possession, but they disappeared faster than Jane Pauley's talk show thereafter.

After getting stopped the first two times they had the ball, the Steelers scored on four consecutive possessions to take a 24-7 lead. The advantage ultimately swelled to 27-7 on a Jeff Reed field goal with 14:48 remaining before the Browns' Leigh Bodden, of

Bringing down Cleveland running back Reuben Droughns are Kimo von Oelhoffen (67) and Joey Porter. *Christopher Horner/Trib Total Media*

Duquesne University, returned a blocked field goal 59 yards to cut it to 27-14 with 4:23 to go. The Steelers added a final score on a 10-yard run by Verron Haynes with 1:53 remaining.

Batch looked far better than he did a week earlier, when he passed for just 65 yards and posted a passer rating of 39.8 in a 20-10 win at Green Bay. He found a rhythm with Ward and the two hooked up late in the second quarter for that historic 15-yard pass.

"Hines deserves this," running back Jerome Bettis said. "He's just a great player and a great teammate."

Ward's catch came one series after Bettis, spelling starter Duce Staley (17 carries for 64 yards), barreled in from a yard out to tie the game at 7-7 with 8:20 left before halftime.

The Steelers added a field goal four plays after Ward's record-breaker to make it 10-7, then used a big defensive play by safety Troy Polamalu and linebacker Joey Porter to set up the clinching touchdown.

Polamalu drilled Browns quarterback Trent Dilfer just as he released a pass and the ball fluttered 15 yards in the air. Porter picked it off and set the Steelers up at the Browns 40. Batch coolly drove the Steelers to the Cleveland 1 with passes of 7, 14, 7, 5 and 6 yards before making a somewhat risky move.

With no timeouts left and the clock running down toward zero, Batch hit Ward on a 6-yard pass at the 1. Instead of spiking the ball for a potential field goal, he raced to the line, clock still ticking, and scored on a quarterback sneak. The play was signaled in from the sideline.

Batch plowed through the right side of the line and scored with six seconds remaining. He was rushed off the field immediately after the play to get the hand looked at by the medical staff.

Tommy Maddox replaced Batch to start the second half, but he didn't have to throw the ball on the first possession. Randle El took care of that on a trick play in which he took a reverse handoff from Staley and lobbed the ball to Ward for a 51-yard score.

Maddox threw just seven times in the second half and completed four passes for 22 yards.

"Tommy's going to be fine," Bettis said. "He has starting experience. He's been there. We'll be fine at quarterback."

	1st	2nd	3rd	4th	Final
Browns	7	0	0	14	21
Steelers	0	17	7	10	34

SCORING SUMMARY

1st

CLE R.Droughns 5-yard run (P.Dawson kick)—10 plays, 66 yards in 5:07.

2nd

PIT J.Bettis 1-yard run (J.Reed kick)—8 plays, 80 yards in 4:39.

PIT J.Reed 42-yard FG—8 plays, 45 yards in 4:06.

PIT C.Batch 1-yard run (J.Reed kick)—9 plays, 40 yards in 1:13.

3rd

PIT H.Ward 51-yard pass from A.Randle El (J.Reed kick)—3 plays, 61 yards in 1:41.

4th

PIT 14:48 J.Reed 33-yard FG—4 plays, 3 yards in 0:53.

CLE L.Bodden 59-yard return of blocked FG (P.Dawson kick).

PIT V.Haynes 10-yard run (J.Reed kick)—5 plays, 29 yards in 2:30.

CLE A.Bryant 9-yard pass from T.Dilfer (P.Dawson kick)—7 plays, 72 yards in 1:32.

TEAM STATS

	BROWNS	STEELERS
1st Downs	16	25
3rd-Down Conversions	5-11	6-13
4th-Down Conversions	1-2	1-2
Punts-Average	4-37.0	2-43.5
Punts-Returns	0-0	3-16
Kickoffs-Returns	7-119	3-52
Int.-Returns	0-0	1-9
Penalties-Yards	9-75	4-30
Fumbles-Lost	1-1	0-0
Time Of Pos.	23:37	36:23
Total Net Yards	303	382
Total Plays	55	68
Net Yards Rushing	61	159
Rushes	19	41
Net Yards Passing	242	223
Comp.-Att.-Int.	17-34-1	18-27-0
Yards Per Pass	6.7	8.3
Sacked-Yards Lost	2-11	0-0
Red Zone Efficiency	2-2-100%	3-5-60%

7 BEN ROETHLISBERGER

Ben Roethlisberger's dream season ended in a nightmare.

Three costly interceptions—one returned 87 yards for a touchdown—contributed largely to a 41-27 loss to the New England Patriots in the 2004 AFC Championship game. Another Steelers season had ended just short of the Super Bowl, and Roethlisberger—who could do nothing wrong during a magical 15-1 season that earned him national acclaim and the Offensive Rookie of the Year award—looked every bit like an overwhelmed rookie.

When it was all said and done, the Steelers quarterback knew exactly who to blame for the postseason failure. Himself.

"Last year, I was kind of like, 'Oh my gosh, I'm so nervous. I'm scared. Here we go, don't make a mistake,'" said Roethlisberger, moments after the Steelers finished the 2005 regular season with a victory over the Detroit Lions, securing the final AFC playoff spot.

"I think I feel more comfortable going into the playoffs now."

Given a second chance to shine in the playoffs, Big Ben didn't disappoint.

All he did was lead the Steelers to three road victories—a feat accomplished just one time before by the 1985 Patriots—against the top three seeds in the AFC: Cincinnati, Indianapolis and Denver. Along the way, he completed 50 of 72 passes for 680 yards, seven touchdowns, one interception and an eye-popping QB rating of 125.8.

Only three quarterbacks, Phil Simms (1986), Joe Montana (1989) and Troy Aikman (1992), had played in three or more playoff games with a higher rating. All three QBs ended their season with a Super Bowl victory.

In one year, Roethlisberger had gone from an overwhelmed rookie to the MVP and unquestionable leader of the Steelers.

"Ben's playing Elway-like," said offensive lineman Kendall Simmons, referring to another Super Bowl winning quarterback, John Elway. "He has this quality that, 'I'm going to get it done, regardless.' He's a second-year guy, but it's like he's been around forever. He just sets the tone for everything."

Added running back Jerome Bettis, "Composed, in control, our leader. He's our guy."

Roethlisberger—at 23 years, 11 months the second-youngest QB every to start a Super Bowl behind Dan Marino in 1984—was taken by the Steelers out of Miami (Ohio) with the 11th overall pick of the 2004 NFL draft. The native of Findlay, Ohio, was expected to spend his first season on the bench behind incumbent starter Tommy Maddox, but saw emergency action in the second week of the season at Baltimore when Maddox was injured.

What happened next is well known ... a 13-0 record as a starter, 17 TDs and an efficient 98.1 QB rating helped the Steelers to just the fourth 15-win regular season in NFL history.

But by the time the playoffs rolled around, the toll of his rookie season began to take an effect on Roethlisberger. His body—and mind—gave out on him.

"I did the whole college season, and the whole training for the draft, then coming here," Roethlisberger said. "It was just two years of non-stop throwing.

"Physically, my arm felt like it was dragging on the floor."

In throwing two interceptions in a near-loss to the New York Jets in the first round, and three more

against the Patriots in the AFC championship, Roethlisberger was clearly affected by nerves and fatigue.

"It made it tough to go out and make the crisp decisions," he said.

Well-rested and admittedly more at ease on the field and in the locker room, Roethlisberger had a solid, though injury-riddled sophomore season. He started 12 games, compiling a 9-3 record and the NFL's third-best passer rating (98.6). He orchestrated the

Steelers' season-ending four-game winning streak that took them from a 7-5 record to an 11-5 mark and the AFC's No. 6 seed.

Wide receiver Hines Ward noticed a big change in Big Ben's demeanor from his rookie season.

"It's more him having fun rather than being quiet," he said. "He's more loose. When a player is loose like that, he tends to go out there and play football and not really worry about each individual thing."

—Jim Rodenbush

STEELERS' ROAD STREAK SNAPPED

BY JOE BENDEL

This was one of those "anything-you-can-do-I-can-do-worse" affairs, an unattractive display of football that Steelers linebacker Clark Haggans described as "funky" and "strange."

He forgot maddening, exasperating and frustrating.

"It was like this: We were jabbing, they were jabbing; we were jabbing, they were jabbing," he said.

Haggans paused, briefly.

"And in the end, they got the final jab in," he said.

The "they" to whom Haggans referred was the Baltimore Ravens, who halted the Steelers' four-game winning streak and ended their own four-game slide with a 16-13 victory in front the largest crowd to watch a football game in this city (70,601).

The Steelers, using a lineup featuring backups at quarterback (Tommy Maddox), left tackle (Trai Essex) and inside linebacker (Clint Kriewaldt), saw their hopes of moving a game ahead of the Cincinnati Bengals in the AFC North disappear when Ravens kicker Matt Stover converted the game-winning, 44-yard field goal with 4:09 left in overtime.

Maddox, 0-2 as a starter this season, oversaw an offense that went 4 of 15 on third downs, averaged just 2.8 yards on 25 rushing attempts, yielded six sacks and posed little threat to the third-ranked defense in the NFL.

Maddox finished 19 of 36 for 230 yards with a touchdown and interception. Not bad statistics, but the veteran quarterback only led the Steelers inside the Ravens 20 twice—and one of those trips occurred after the Steelers recovered a fumble at the Baltimore 20.

He confirmed afterward that there were communication issues with the sideline in getting plays in on time, forcing him to use his final timeout of regulation with 13:39 to go.

If that wasn't bad enough, the Ravens were pinning their ears back and attacking Maddox at every turn.

"Our goal was to get in his face and force him to make decisions," Ravens defensive end Jarret Johnson said. "I think we were able to accomplish that."

Steelers No. 1 quarterback Ben Roethlisberger, who missed his third consecutive game while healing from arthroscopic surgery on his right knee, is hopeful he'll be back next Monday night against the undefeated Colts in Indianapolis, where, perhaps, he'll resurrect the sputtering offense.

"I'm going to do everything I can (to be able to play)," Roethlisberger said in the aftermath of the Steelers' first road loss in 12 games.

With the loss, the Steelers (7-3) remain tied with the Bengals (7-3) for the top spot in the AFC North. The Bengals play host to the Ravens (3-7) next Sunday before traveling to Heinz Field for a showdown with the Steelers on Dec. 4.

Pittsburgh backup quarterback Tommy Maddox has the ball knocked away by Baltimore's Jarret Johnson during the fourth quarter. The Ravens recovered the fumble as the Steelers suffered a 16-13 overtime loss. *Philip G. Pavely/Trib Total Media*

Stopped just shy of the line of scrimmage, Steelers running back Jerome Bettis is dragged down by Maake Kemoeatu and Jarret Johnson (95). Bettis rushed twice for zero yards in the overtime loss. *Philip G. Pavely/Trib Total Media*

"We'll look at this and learn from this," said Steelers wideout Hines Ward, who finished with six catches for 81 yards. "It's really a six-game season for us. We're right in the thick of things. When you have the opportunity to win games, you have to seize it."

Added free safety Chris Hope, "We didn't help ourselves here today. You always want to control your own fate and not have to rely on anybody. Fortunately, we still get to play the Bengals and Colts, so we can get things together and make things happen for ourselves."

Entering yesterday's game, the Ravens hadn't scored a touchdown in 11 consecutive quarters and just once in the previous 19 (against the Steelers in Week 7). But they ended that string of futility when quarterback Kyle Boller (21 of 36 for 163 yards with a touchdown and interception) hit wideout Randy Hymes for a 3-yard touchdown with 6:09 remaining before halftime. That gave them a 10-3 lead, which eventually turned into a 13-6 advantage at intermission.

It was then that the Ravens appeared to find the swagger that had eluded them the previous four games.

"We definitely felt like that was a team we weren't supposed to let hang around, because if you let them hang around, their confidence is going to build," Steelers linebacker Joey Porter said. "That's what happened. If we go out there and jump on them early, it's possible that they just quit, but we went into halftime losing and their crowd got into it."

The Steelers found just enough offense in the second half to tie it, 13-13, with 5:15 remaining. Tailback Willie Parker added the final touches with an 11-yard touchdown reception on a screen pass from Maddox.

The Steelers had the ball twice in overtime, but failed to get into scoring position. The Ravens, following a 13-yard punt return by B.J. Sams, then drove 30 yards on the winning drive, aided by a questionable facemask penalty on Steelers linebacker Larry Foote that gave them second-and-1 at the Steelers 35. Four plays later, Stover hit the game-winner.

	1st	2nd	3rd	4th	OT	Final
Steelers	0	6	0	7	0	13
Ravens	0	13	0	0	3	16

SCORING SUMMARY

1st
No scoring.

2nd
BAL M. Stover 47-yard FG—10 plays, 38 yards in 3:46.
PIT J. Reed 44-yard FG—8 plays, 50 yards in 4:24.
BAL R. Hymes 3-yard pass from K. Boller (M. Stover kick)—8 plays, 47 yards in 3:44.
PIT J. Reed 37-yard FG—4 plays, 1 yard in 0:55.
BAL M. Stover 25-yard FG—10 plays, 61 yards in 4:15.

3rd
No scoring.

4th
PIT W.Parker 11-yard pass from T.Maddox (J.Reed kick)—7 plays, 85 yards in 4:29.

OT
BAL M.Stover 44-yard FG—10 plays, 30 yards in 4:00.

TEAM STATS

	STEELERS	RAVENS
1st Downs	17	18
3rd-Down Conversions	4-15	7-20
4th-Down Conversions	0-1	0-0
Punts-Average	8-41.9	8-43.8
Punts-Returns	4-12	5-54
Kickoffs-Returns	5-71	4-130
Int.-Returns	1-26	1-0
Penalties-Yards	10-62	11-70
Fumbles-Lost	1-1	1-1
Time Of Pos.	28:48	31:12
Total Net Yards	282	241
Total Plays	69	79
Net Yards Rushing	70	104
Rushes	25	38
Net Yards Passing	212	137
Comp.-Att.-Int.	21-38-1	21-36-1
Yards Per Pass	4.8	3.3
Sacked-Yards Lost	6-34	5-26
Red Zone Efficiency	1-3-33%	1-2-50%

DOMED FROM THE START

BY JOE BENDEL

There was the missed 41-yard field goal by Jeff Reed. The late second-quarter interception thrown by Ben Roethlisberger. The countless false-start penalties. And the failed onside kick to open the second half.

All of these things conspired against the Steelers in 26-7 loss to the Indianapolis Colts at the RCA Dome, but it's hardly fair to explain their second consecutive defeat by pointing only to these instances.

The Colts entered as 8-point favorites and looked every bit like a Super Bowl team.

The Steelers were nothing more than victim No. 11 for these Colts, who upped their record to 11-0, as they continued their quest to become the second team in league history to go through an entire season undefeated.

Even on a night when All-Pro quarterback Peyton Manning wasn't his dominant self (15 of 25 for 245 yards with two touchdowns and an interception) the Colts, buoyed by a boisterous crowd of 57,442, found a way to keep their streak alive.

"They beat us all the way around," Steelers running back Jerome Bettis said. "They were the better team. They dominated from the word, 'Go.' It was a frustrating night—all the way across the board."

Added safety Troy Polamalu, "They're the best team in the league. They proved it."

The Colts had been averaging a shade below 40 points the previous three games, but thanks to a defense that stifled the Steelers (197 total yards; 86 rushing), there was no need to get into a shootout, as they'd done the previous week in a 45-37 victory over the Bengals.

The Steelers dropped to 7-4—a full game behind AFC North leader Cincinnati, which next plays at Heinz Field. If the playoffs started today, the Steelers would not be one of the six representatives from the AFC in the postseason.

That leaves them with little margin for error as they play their final five games against the Bengals, Bears (8-3), at the Vikings (6-5), at the Browns (4-7) and at home against the Lions (4-7).

"The good thing is, if we win next week, we still control our fate," cornerback Deshea Townsend said.

Quarterback Ben Roethlisberger returned last night after missing the previous three games with a right knee injury, but he couldn't produce the magic that had helped him lead the Steelers to victories in 18 of his previous 19 regular-season starts. He went 17 of 26 for 133 yards with a touchdown and two interceptions, the final of which, with 5:31 remaining, put a stamp on this forgettable loss.

The Steelers had hoped to become streak-busters, but they saw a streak of their own get thrown by the

Ganging up on Pittsburgh quarterback Ben Roethlisberger are Dwight Freeney (93) and Josh Thomas (91). *Christopher Horner/Trib Total Media*

wayside. Edgerrin James ran for 124 tough yards on 29 carries, becoming the first running back in 23 regular-season games to eclipse the century mark against the Steelers.

It didn't take the Colts long to set the tempo in this one, as Manning hit a streaking Marvin Harrison for an 80-yard score on the Colts' first offensive play. Harrison used a slight stutter-step move to freeze Steelers cornerback Ike Taylor, then sprinted down

"They beat us all the way around. They were the better team. They dominated from the word, 'Go.' It was a frustrating night—all the way across the board."

—RUNNING BACK JEROME BETTIS

The Colts' Edgerrin James gains yardage, but Troy Polamalu closes in behind him during the third quarter. *Philip G. Pavely/Trib Total Media*

the sideline as Manning deftly laid the ball into his arms.

Just like that, it was 7-0 Colts.

The Steelers went backwards on their first two possessions, going for minus-7 yards, and the Colts kept plowing forward, adding a field goal by Mike Vanderjagt (who went 4 of 4) for a 10-0 lead.

The momentum looked as if it might shift on the Colts' next possession, when Polamalu intercepted a pass by Manning and returned it 36 yards to the Indianapolis 7. After back-to-back false-starts by Steelers guard Kendall Simmons, Roethlisberger hit Hines Ward for a 12-yard score that cut the margin to 10-7 at 1:14 of the first quarter.

Reed missed a field goal on the Steelers next possession that would have tied it at 10-10, and that was the last opportunity for the Steelers.

The Colts added two more field goals to close the half, the second of which came after Roethlisberger was intercepted with 15 seconds to go by safety Mike Doss. Indianapolis held a 16-7 advantage at the half.

Then came the onside kick, one of the more crucial decisions by coach Bill Cowher, who said he was trying to create a "spark" for his team. The Colts did not seem surprised, and Matt Giordano recovered at the Indianapolis 37.

Manning needed only seven plays to make the Steelers pay, the final of which was a 12-yard scoring pass to tight end Bryan Fletcher that made it 23-7 less than four minutes into the third quarter.

That spelled doom for the Steelers, because Colts coach Tony Dungy is now 51-0 when his teams have leads of 14 points or more.

Dungy's Colts did what few teams have done against the Steelers—beat them up physically. The Colts rolled up 366 yards, 127 of which came on the ground.

"I think we were going to be physical and tough and not back down," Dungy said.

	1st	2nd	3rd	4th	Final
Steelers	7	0	0	0	7
Colts	10	6	7	3	26

SCORING SUMMARY

1st

IND M. Harrison 80-yard pass from P. Manning (M. Vanderjagt kick)—1 play, 80 yards in 0:10.

IND M. Vanderjagt 29-yard FG—9 plays, 45 yards in 5:06.

PIT H. Ward 12-yard pass from B. Roethlisberger (J. Reed kick)—3 plays, 7 yards in 2:00.

2nd

IND M. Vanderjagt 48-yard FG—4 plays, 6 yards in 0:49.

IND M. Vanderjagt 44-yard FG—3 plays, 19 yards in 0:15.

3rd

IND B. Fletcher 12-yard pass from P. Manning (M. Vanderjagt kick)—7 plays, 37 yards in 3:13.

4th

IND M. Vanderjagt 28-yard FG—8 plays, 26 yards in 3:53.

TEAM STATS

	STEELERS	COLTS
1st Downs	10	17
3rd-Down Conversions	4-13	5-13
4th-Down Conversions	0-1	0-0
Punts-Average	6-46.0	5-45.8
Punts-Returns	1-19	3-36
Kickoffs-Returns	6-119	1-14
Int.-Returns	1-36	2-8
Penalties-Yards	10-62	12-106
Fumbles-Lost	0-0	1-0
Time Of Pos.	29:13	30:47
Total Net Yards	197	366
Total Plays	54	59
Net Yards Rushing	86	127
Rushes	25	32
Net Yards Passing	111	239
Comp.-Att.-Int.	17-26-2	15-25-1
Sacked-Yards Lost	3-22	2-6
Red Zone Efficiency	0-0-0%	0-0-0%

BENGALS TAKE CONTROL

BY JOE BENDEL

The thunderous thumping coming from the Cincinnati sideline was the sound of racing Bengals heartbeats.

"Could you hear it?" receiver/return specialist Tab Perry said. "I was scared as heck."

"It wasn't just my heart you were hearing; I was saying, 'Oh (shoot),'" said wideout T.J. Houshmandzadeh.

The Bengals finally breathed a sigh of relief when Steelers safety Troy Polamalu narrowly missed intercepting a Carson Palmer pass for what might have been the game-tying touchdown with a little less than three minutes remaining.

The Bengals survived to emerge with a 38-31 victory at Heinz Field.

"If he would have taken that back for a touchdown. The momentum would have switched right there, and then, it would have been like, 'Here we go again. ...'" Bengals linebacker Caleb Miller said.

That's what might have happened in the past, when the Bengals were the Bungles and they were also-rans in the AFC North Division. But Polamalu's near-miss represented a role reversal for a Steelers team that always seemed to find a way to put a dagger in Cincinnati.

The Bengals (9-3) are in firm command of the AFC North, two games ahead of the Steelers (7-5) with four games to go. The Steelers, riding a three-game losing streak, could still win the division if the Bengals struggled, and they figure out how to win again.

But the Steelers no longer control their own destiny.

"We know that our back is against the wall," Steelers tailback Duce Staley said. "And any time you got a wounded animal with his back against the wall, he either comes out fighting or he dies. So, don't expect for this team to die, because we're not going to."

The Steelers play at home Sunday against Chicago (9-3), which is riding an eight-game winning streak, at Minnesota (7-5), at Cleveland (4-8) and at home against Detroit (4-8) in the regular-season finale.

A loss in any of those games would likely end their playoff hopes. If the season ended today, they would not make the postseason.

"Even if we win our last four, 11-5 might not make it," wide receiver Hines Ward said. "But we can't think about it. If you look too far into the playoff (scenarios), you're putting added pressure on instead of going out and playing."

The Steelers had a chance to pull even with the Bengals in the division yesterday and take control of the division, by virtue of their Week 6 victory over the Bengals. But they turned the ball over four times, failed

Cincinnati's Rudi Johnson dives over the pylon into the endzone to score the game-winning touchdown during the fourth quarter against the Steelers. *Christopher Horner/Trib Total Media*

to stifle Palmer (22 of 38 for 227 yards with three touchdowns) and committed back-to-back penalties on their final possession in the game's waning moments that essentially put their postseason hopes on hold.

"I told (the team), at this point, just play it out, whatever happens, happens," said coach Bill Cowher, who has beaten the Bengals in 20 of 28 meetings.

The Steelers outgained the Bengals, 474-324, won the battle of time of possession, 33:18-26:42, and produced seven more first downs than the Bengals.

Pittsburgh wideout Cedrick Wilson hauls in a reception in the fourth quarter as Cincinnati defenders Kevin Kaesviham (34) and Tory James apply coverage. *Philip G. Pavely/Trib Total Media*

Even injured quarterback Ben Roethlisberger produced big numbers (29 of 41 for 386 yards and three scores), but perhaps his injured thumb conspired against him in throwing a regular-season high three interceptions against a Bengals team that leads the NFL in give-away, take-away ratio at plus-24.

The Bengals did not turn the ball over, while turning two of the four Steelers turnovers into 14 points.

"That's the tough part, we gave it to them so many times, and we still could have won this game," Ward said.

"We know that our back is against the wall. And any time you got a wounded animal with his back against the wall, he either comes out fighting or he dies. So, don't expect for this team to die, because we're not going to."

—TAILBACK DUCE STALEY

	1st	2nd	3rd	4th	Final
Bengals	7	14	10	7	38
Steelers	14	3	7	7	31

SCORING SUMMARY

1st
PIT   J. Bettis 1-yard run (J. Reed kick)—8 plays, 68 yards in 4:34.
CIN   T. Houshmandzadeh 43-yard pass from C. Palmer (S. Graham kick)—4 plays, 74 yards in 1:23.
PIT   Q. Morgan 25-yard pass from B. Roethlisberger (J. Reed kick)—7 plays, 72 yards in 3:09.

2nd 14
CIN   R. Kelly 1-yard pass from C. Palmer (S. Graham kick)—11 plays, 53 yards in 5:05.
CIN   T. Houshmandzadeh 6-yard pass from C. Palmer (S. Graham kick)—6 plays, 22 yards in 2:03.
PIT   J. Reed 23-yard FG—8 plays, 64 yards in 2:52.

3rd
CIN   S. Graham 30-yard FG—9 plays, 51 yards in 3:59.
PIT   H. Ward 20-yard pass from B. Roethlisberger (J. Reed kick)—4 plays, 58 yards in 1:56.
CIN   R. Johnson 1-yard run (S. Graham kick)—2 plays, 4 yards in 1:08.

4th
CIN   R. Johnson 14-yard run (S. Graham kick)—6 plays, 49 yards in 2:50.
PIT   H. Ward 6-yard pass from B. Roethlisberger (J. Reed kick)—10 plays, 72 yards in 3:10.

TEAM STATS

	BENGALS	STEELERS
1st Downs	21	28
3rd-Down Conversions	6-14	6-13
4th-Down Conversions	0-1	0-1
Punts-Average	5-46.8	3-32.0
Punts-Returns	1-3	2-8
Kickoffs-Returns	5-197	6-136
Int.-Returns	3-58	0-0
Penalties-Yards	4-30	7-70
Fumbles-Lost	0-0	4-1
Time Of Pos.	26:42	33:18
Total Net Yards	324	474
Total Plays	64	71
Net Yards Rushing	102	95
Rushes	25	28
Net Yards Passing	222	379
Comp.-Att.-Int.	22-38-0	29-41-3
Sacked-Yards Lost	1-5	2-7
Red Zone Efficiency	4-6-66%	2-3-66%

STEELERS BACK IN THE HUNT

BY JOE BENDEL

Desperate times called for devastating measures for the Steelers.

So, they turned the clock back to long, long ago—four weeks, to be precise—and returned to their bone-jarring brand of football in pummeling the Chicago Bears, 21-9, on Sunday at snow-covered Heinz Field.

"We lived to fight another day," coach Bill Cowher said.

This streak-snapping win—the Steelers had lost three in a row; the Bears had won eight—showcased a rejuvenated Steelers offensive line that scattered the league's No. 1 defense like flimsy bowling pins.

And, the Steelers held the ball for 37 minutes, 19 seconds, including 22-plus in the second half.

"We got back on track," said center Jeff Hartings, who voiced his concerns about the team's confidence after a 38-31 loss to Cincinnati a week earlier that pretty much knocked them out of the AFC North title hunt and damaged their postseason aspirations. "I think, coming off a season where you win 15 games (as the Steelers did in '04), you kind of forget what got you there. I'll never question our effort, but we weren't executing the way we should have been. And you get your execution from good practices on Wednesday, Thursday and Friday. We probably didn't do that the whole year until this week."

The Steelers (8-5) remain in the hunt for one of the two AFC wild-card berths, along with Jacksonville (9-4), Kansas City (8-5) and San Diego (8-5), with three games to go. Their remaining games are at Minnesota (8-5), which has won six in a row, at Cleveland (4-9) and at home against Detroit.

"We're a desperate football team, and we're going to play like that for the rest of the season," said Bettis, who reeled off a 39-yard run and scored twice. "Hopefully, that will give us the sense of urgency that we've been missing."

Bettis, who might be playing his final NFL season, was the beneficiary of an offensive line that showed its agility in getting out on screens, keeping Bears defensive ends Alex Brown and Adewale Ogunleye from Roethlisberger. Rookie Trai Essex and two-year vet Max Starks were solid at the tackle spots.

"I don't think the other guys were riding my coattails," said guard Alan Faneca, who set the tone early by crushing Bears defensive end Ian Scott and springing Parker loose on a 45-yard screen that led to the Steelers first score. "Our offense likes to use me a lot in movement, getting me out on the edge, pulling and leading screens. Sometimes, it isn't there. Today, it was there and I got a chance to do that."

Faneca laid a key block in sending Hines Ward on a 12-yard touchdown on the Steelers' first possession

Steelers quarterback Ben Roethlisberger gets a pass off before he is reached by Bears defender Hunter Hillenmeyer during the third quarter.
Philip G. Pavely/Trib Total Media

(Ward plowed through two Bears to get into the end zone), then helped create lanes for Bettis on his touchdown runs of 1 yard (second quarter) and 5 yards (third quarter).

"Steelers football," Essex said, smiling. "Snow ... Running the football. ... Winning at home."

Ogunleye, who entered with nine sacks but barely sniffed Roethlisberger, did not want to concede that this Bears defense, which had allowed 20 or more points just twice before, was outmuscled.

"Early on, they didn't want to see us face to face," he said. "They didn't want to go head-up with us. So,

they did a lot of screens and stuff like that. They didn't want to try to out-physical us. Once they got that lead, that's all they had to do. We kind of played into their hands today."

That's typically what happens when the Steelers are playing Steelers football.

"It was our type of game," Hartings said. "But still, we have to stay focused, remember where we were. We can't afford any more slip-ups."

Steelers running back Willie Parker is knocked out of bounds at the 1-yard line by Chicago's Brandon McGowan. The play set up the Steelers' first touchdown. *Philip G. Pavely/Trib Total Media*

	1st	2nd	3rd	4th	Final
Bears	3	0	0	6	9
Steelers	7	7	7	0	21

SCORING SUMMARY

1st

PIT   H. Ward 14-yard pass from B. Roethlisberger (J. Reed kick)—5 plays, 66 yards, in 2:52.

CHI   R. Gould 29-yard FG—14 plays, 63 yards in 6:46.

2nd

PIT   J. Bettis 1-yard run (J. Reed kick)—9 plays, 73 yards in 5:19.

3rd

PIT   J. Bettis 5-yard run (J. Reed kick)—12 plays, 52 yards in 7:01.

4th

CHI   T. Jones 1-yard run (kick failed, wide left)—3 plays, 71 yards in 1:22.

TEAM STATS

	BEARS	STEELERS
1st Downs	15	20
3rd-Down Conversions	3-13	7-14
4th-Down Conversions	1-2	0-1
Punts-Average	7-39.9	6-40.0
Punts-Returns	4-26	6-42
Kickoffs-Returns	4-54	3-59
Int.-Returns	0-0	0-0
Penalties-Yards	1-5	7-55
Fumbles-Lost	2-0	4-0
Time Of Pos.	22:41	37:19
Total Net Yards	268	363
Total Plays	56	66
Net Yards Rushing	83	190
Rushes	18	46
Net Yards Passing	185	173
Comp.-Att.-Int.	17-35-0	13-20-0
Yards Per Pass	4.9	8.6
Sacked-Yards Lost	3-22	0-0
Red Zone Efficiency	1-2-50%	3-3-100%

Celebrating his second touchdown against the Bears is Pittsburgh running back Jerome Bettis. *Christopher Horner/Trib Total Media*

"Steelers football ... Snow ... Running the football ... Winning at home."

—TACKLE TRAI ESSEX

43 TROY POLAMALU

In just three seasons, Troy Polamalu has become the main man in the Steelers' secondary.

Make that the mane man.

His long locks spilling out from under his helmet have made Polamalu a fan favorite at Heinz Field. His speed, abandon and gut instinct have made him arguably the best strong safety in the NFL.

Polamalu—the No. 16 overall pick by the Steelers in 2003 out of Southern California—recorded 92 tackles and two interceptions in 2005, earning first-team All-Pro honors and a Pro Bowl starting spot. Beyond the statistics, Polamalu takes pride in being a destructive force on defense.

"That's where I get my greatest satisfaction," he said.

Polamalu, 24, played a key role in helping the Steelers to three consecutive road victories and a berth in Super Bowl XL against the Seattle Seahawks.

In the wild-card round against the Cincinnati Bengals, he had six tackles, one tackle for a loss, a half sack, one pass defended and one interception.

Against the top-seeded Indianapolis Colts the next week, he notched seven tackles, two passes defended—and one well-publicized interception that was erroneously overturned by the officials. Polamalu confused Colts quarterback Peyton Manning at nearly every turn, making the two-time MVP fret about his whereabouts on the field.

Polamalu's physical style helped produce a big play just before halftime. Polamalu teamed with outside linebacker Clark Haggans to stop running back Edgerrin James at the Steelers' 2-yard line on a third-and-goal. The Colts had to settle for a field goal and a 14-3 deficit.

"Troy has to be accounted for on every play," inside linebacker James Farrior said. "He's such a dynamic player and can do so many things that teams really have to know where he is at all times and know what he's doing."

"The Steelers do a great job with their scheme of making it very tough to figure out where he's at," said Denver coach Mike Shanahan before Polamalu recorded six tackles against the Broncos in the AFC title game. "The rest is him making plays. He's sideline-to-sideline. There aren't too many times when he's not involved with the play. You can't say that about many players in the National Football League. He plays with one of the highest motors I've ever seen."

Count Broncos quarterback Jake Plummer among Polamalu's biggest fans.

"Just watching film and the couple of games I've seen him in this year, he's a fun player," Plummer said. "He flies around. I'm not a strong safety, but if I did play that position, that's the way I would want to play. Running around, flying around, just doing some crazy stuff and making plays."

Offenses try to keep Polamalu from making plays. Good luck said linebacker Larry Foote.

"I'm sure the quarterback will try to know where he's at, but we put him all over the place," he said. "You can't design an offense away from him because he can line up one place and go another.

"He's an animal. He can do it all—stop the run, play the pass, cover receivers. That's what separates him from other safeties."

Polamalu, 5-foot-10, 212 pounds, failed to crack the Steelers' starting lineup in his rookie season, recording 23 tackles, two sacks and a forced fumble.

His breakthrough season came in 2004, when as the starting strong safety he notched 94 tackles, one sack and five interceptions, one which was returned

for a touchdown. For his efforts, he was named a second team All-Pro.

Steelers coach Bill Cowher said Polamalu stands out because of quickness and instincts.

"He can time things up and be very explosive," he said. "It looks sometimes like he's walking and not moving, but can go from point A to point B very quickly. He's a very sudden player, and I think that's

The Steelers entered this season hoping for even more from Polamalu, and designed their scheme to make that happen.

"Troy's growing as a player, just like some of the other guys are, and they're doing more things with him," Steelers offensive coordinator Ken Whisenhunt said.

—Jim Rodenbush

DEFENSE TAKES OVER IN STEELERS' WIN

BY JOE BENDEL

The confrontation was unmercifully lopsided: Steelers nose tackle Casey Hampton vs. Minnesota Vikings center Cory Withrow.

"I have to admit, I was surprised they tried to block me with one man," Hampton said, smiling.

The operative word here is "try." Because Hampton plowed through the stumbling Withrow like he was made of paper, and gift-wrapped Michael Bennett for Steelers linebacker Larry Foote, who threw the shell-shocked running back for a safety.

The play not only put the finishing touches on an 18-3 victory, but also underscored the defensive dominance displayed by Hampton, Foote and Co. in a game that significantly improved the Steelers' playoff chances.

"We couldn't have scripted the ending any better," Foote said. "It was a powerful statement, a powerful finish. This was Steelers football. It was ... Steelers defense."

Because of that defense—which yielded 52 rushing yards, forced two turnovers and held the Vikings to a field goal in four trips to the red zone—the Steelers (9-5) remained strongly in the hunt for one of the AFC's two wild-card spots.

But they still need help.

The best-case scenario for the Steelers is to win their final two games at Cleveland (5-9) on Christmas Eve and at home against Detroit (4-10) on New Year's Day, and hope for Jacksonville (10-4), which holds the first wild-card position, to keep on winning.

Reason being, the Steelers can't afford to get into a three-way tie with Jacksonville and San Diego (9-5). If all three end up 11-5, the Steelers are the odd team out based on conference record—they would be 7-5, San Diego, 9-3 and Jacksonville, 8-4—even though they own a head-to-head victory over San Diego.

If the Steelers and the Chargers end up tied at 11-5, and Jacksonville finishes 12-4 (the Jags close with Tennessee and Houston), the head-to-head tiebreaker would come into play between the Chargers and the Steelers. The Steelers win out in that instance.

Simply put, if the Steelers and Jaguars win their final two, the team from Pittsburgh is headed to the postseason.

"The only thing I can worry about right now is Cleveland," coach Bill Cowher said. "I'm not going to dwell on this game very much, and I'm not going to look at anything beyond that. When you do that, it clears your mind. There's not a whole lot you have to think about."

The Steelers might want to think about calling themselves streak busters, because they've done just that the past two weeks. They ended Chicago's eight-

As Joey Porter (55) stops the Vikings' progress, Aaron Smith (91) celebrates the tackle. *Chaz Palla/Trib Total Media*

game streak at Heinz Field a week earlier and shattered the Vikings' six-game streak yesterday.

Now, they're on a run of their own. They've won two in a row after losing three straight.

"We never thought we were out of it, even when we were losing," Hampton said. "Our goal always was, and is, to win the Super Bowl. But it's at the point right now where we just have to worry about us. One game at a time. Whatever happens, happens. Deal with it."

The Vikings, who were fighting for their playoff lives, feasted mostly on losing teams during their streak, and were not up to the task against a Steelers team that got efficient play from quarterback Ben Roethlisberger (10 of 15 for 149 yards with a 99.0

Pittsburgh's James Farrior (51) goes for a low tackle, while strong safety Troy Polamalu (43) fills the gap. *Chaz Palla/Trib Total Media*

rating), solid play from the running game (142 yards), clock domination (36:48 to 23:12) and timely play from the special teams (Antwaan Randle returned a punt 72 yards that led to the game's first touchdown and a 10-3 halftime lead; Kimo von Oelhoffen blocked a field goal that prevented the Vikings from making it 10-6 to open the second half; and safety Tyrone Carter recovered a fumble on a kickoff that led to a field goal).

Then, there was the defense.

The Vikings, on the strength of a controversial fumble by Randle El on a punt, had a first-and-goal at the Steelers' 3 midway through the first quarter, but only mustered a field goal. The key play was a hit on Vikings running back Ciatrick Fason by linebacker James Harrison on third-and-1.

The tone was set from there.

The Vikings drove to the Steelers' 5 on their next possession, only to have typically dependable quarterback Brad Johnson throw a desperation, two-handed pass toward wideout Koren Robinson that caught Robinson off-guard and tipped into the arms of Steelers linebacker Joey Porter for an interception.

"I didn't know what was going on there," Robinson said. "I didn't know it was coming."

Later, cornerback Deshea Townsend intercepted Johnson in the end zone on the Vikings final possession of the first half, then, von Oelhoffen blocked a 32-yard field goal attempt, after the Vikings reached the 15.

"When you keep losing opportunities, you start to feel it a little," Robinson said. "We lost too many opportunities against a good team. You just can't do those things against a defense like this and think you have a chance to win."

	1st	2nd	3rd	4th	Final
Steelers	3	7	6	2	18
Vikings	3	0	0	0	3

SCORING SUMMARY

1st
PIT J. Reed 21-yard FG—7 plays, 72 yards in 3:53.
MIN P. Edinger 20-yard FG—4 plays, 1 yard in 1:26.

2nd
PIT B. Roethlisberger 3-yard run (J. Reed kick)—6 plays, 14 yards in 3:12.

3rd
PIT J. Reed 41-yard FG—9 plays, 63 yards in 6:11.
PIT J. Reed 26-yard FG—5 plays, 21 yards in 3:13.

4th
PIT M. Bennett tackled in end zone by L. Foote (J. Porter for a safety).

TEAM STATS

	STEELERS	VIKINGS
1st Downs	14	11
3rd-Down Conversions	5-15	3-12
4th-Down Conversions	1-1	0-0
Punts-Average	6-47.0	6-44.5
Punts-Returns	5-85	4-41
Kickoffs-Returns	3-56	5-83
Int.-Returns	2-0	0-0
Penalties-Yards	12-129	13-95
Fumbles-Lost	2-1	3-1
Time Of Pos.	36:48	23:12
Total Net Yards	275	185
Total Plays	58	49
Net Yards Rushing	142	54
Rushes	39	17
Net Yards Passing	133	131
Comp.-Att.-Int.	10-15-0	16-30-2
Sacked-Yards Lost	4-16	2-12
Red Zone Efficiency	1-4-25%	0-4-0%

"We couldn't have scripted the ending any better. It was a powerful statement, a powerful finish. This was Steelers football. It was ... Steelers defense."

—LINEBACKER LARRY FOOTE

HOLIDAY HAMMERING

BY JOE BENDEL

'T was the day before Christmas and all through the Pound, not a single fan was stirring ... unless he or she happened to be sporting black and gold.

The Steelers arrived here and ruined Christmas for a Browns team that had hoped to play the role of playoff spoiler against their longtime rivals.

Final score: Steelers 41, Browns 0.

This one was over in an instant, as the Browns looked like they started early on the eggnog. The Steelers scored on their first three possessions, raced to a 20-0 halftime lead and rode a defense, led by inspired Pro Bowl linebacker Joey Porter, that held the Browns to one first down and 22 yards in the first half. Porter sacked Cleveland rookie quarterback Charlie Frye three times, pushing his season total to 10.5, tying his career high.

The final moments of the game were played out to just a few thousand fans, most of them waving Terrible Towels and watching Steelers linebacker Larry Foote planting Aaron Shea at the Browns 3-yard line on the final play.

Steelers quarterback Ben Roethlisberger got things started by slicing and dicing the Browns as if they were holiday ham, going 13 of 20 for 226 yards with a touchdown, and Willie Parker became the first Steelers player to reach 1,000 rushing yards since 2001.

Parker hit the milestone in grand fashion—on an 80-yard scoring burst in the third quarter that not only broke the game wide open, but also represented the longest by a Steelers running back since Frenchy Fuqua went 85 yards against the Philadelphia Eagles in 1970.

Jerome Bettis scored the game's first touchdown from 2 yards out, wide receiver Hines Ward followed with a 7-yard scoring reception, his 11th of the season, Verron Haynes contributed a 15-yard touchdown run, Quincy Morgan hauled in a 31-yarder from backup quarterback Charlie Batch and Jeff Reed went 2 of 2 on field goals.

But the holiday celebration did not end there for the Steelers, who won for the third consecutive time and upped their record to 10-5.

They received word immediately afterward that the Kansas City Chiefs sent them a neatly wrapped Christmas gift by beating San Diego and dropping the Chargers to 9-6. That means all the Steelers must do is defeat the Detroit Lions (5-10) at Heinz Field and they'll punch their ticket as a wild-card participant in the playoffs.

"Next week is a playoff game," said coach Bill Cowher, who's won 11 of the last 12 against the Browns. "If we lose, that's it. No playoffs and we go home."

Steelers receiver Cedrick Wilson catches a long pass in front of the Browns' Chris Crocker during the first quarter at Cleveland Browns Stadium.
Christopher Horner/Trib Total Media

The Steelers' defense of Clark Haggans (53) and Casey Hampton (98) pressures Browns quarterback Charlie Frye during the third quarter. The Steelers dominated the Browns, shutting them out 41-0. *Philip G. Pavely/Trib Total Media*

The fact that the Steelers control their playoff fate after dropping three consecutive games in Weeks 10-12 not only speaks to the ever-changing dynamics of the NFL, but also to their ability to bounce back from adversity.

"But it's not over," right tackle Max Starks said. "We have another battle ahead of us."

Before the Browns (5-10) knew what had hit them yesterday, Roethlisberger was picking them apart, completing passes to Antwaan Randle El (20 yards), Cedrick Wilson (17) and tight end Heath Miller (21) on the opening drive. Bettis finished things off with three consecutive runs, the final of which saw him carry Browns linebacker Ben Taylor into the end zone.

The Browns went three-and-out on the ensuing possession (a frequent occurrence yesterday) and Roethlisberger continued his assault, going 3 of 3 for 58 yards, including a thread-the-needle 7-yarder to Ward, who snatched the ball over the Browns' Ray Mickens.

Roethlisberger's passer rating at the end of the first quarter was a perfect 158.3, as he went 7 of 8 (he missed on his first attempt) for 162 yards with the touchdown. He had a long pass of 49 yards to Wilson.

The Browns, who entered with the league's 23rd-ranked offense, had little hope of a comeback once Reed hit a 26-yard field goal that pushed the Steelers ahead 17-0 before the half. The Steelers are 98-1-1 under Cowher when they hold a lead of 11 points or more.

"We control our destiny now," Cowher said. "That's all that counts."

	1st	2nd	3rd	4th	Final
Steelers	14	6	14	7	41
Browns	0	0	0	0	0

SCORING SUMMARY

1st

PIT J. Bettis 2-yard run (J. Reed kick)—11 plays, 84 yards in 5:51.

PIT H. Ward 7-yard pass from B. Roethlisberger (J. Reed kick)—6 plays, 63 yards in 3:08.

2nd

PIT J. Reed 26-yard FG—6 plays, 55 yards in 2:31.

PIT J. Reed 31-yard FG—8 plays, 38 yards in 3:45.

3rd

PIT W. Parker 80-yard run (J. Reed kick)—1 play, 80 yards in 0:12.

PIT V. Haynes 15-yard run (J. Reed kick)—2 plays, 15 yards in 0:45.

4th

PIT Q. Morgan 31-yard pass from C. Batch (J. Reed kick)—7 plays, 56 yards in 5:13.

TEAM STATS

	STEELERS	BROWNS
1st Downs	20	12
3rd-Down Conversions	7-12	2-16
4th-Down Conversions	0-0	3-5
Punts-Average	3-42.0	8-41.9
Punts-Returns	5-52	1-8
Kickoffs-Returns	1-22	8-133
Int.-Returns	0-0	0-0
Penalties-Yards	3-30	4-25
Fumbles-Lost	1-1	5-1
Time Of Pos.	31:39	28:21
Total Net Yards	457	178
Total Plays	58	66
Net Yards Rushing	209	55
Rushes	35	19
Net Yards Passing	248	123
Comp.-Att.-Int.	14-21-0	20-39-0
Sacked-Yards Lost	2-9	8-60
Red Zone Efficiency	3-5-60%	0-2-0%

READY TO GO

BY JOE BENDEL

S teelers quarterback Ben Roethlisberger is acting like a man seeking redemption, like a man on a Super Bowl mission.

"I think I feel more comfortable going into the playoffs now," said Roethlisberger, moments after the Steelers defeated the Detroit Lions, 35-21, and secured a meeting with Cincinnati Bengals in the first round of the playoffs at Paul Brown Stadium. "Last year, I was kind of, 'Oh my gosh, I'm so nervous, I'm scared, here we go, don't make a mistake.'"

Although he is just 23 and only a year removed from his rookie season, which concluded with five postseason interceptions, three of which came in the AFC title loss to New England at Heinz Field, Roethlisberger feels he has come of age.

"I'm not going to go out and play not to make a mistake this year," Roethlisberger said. "I'm going to go out to win football games and play as good as I can to help this team win. It came from a feeling like (I) lost it last year for the team, for making mistakes and not wanting to do it again and not wanting to make the same mistakes twice.

"I think it's a journey, growing up and getting older."

The Steelers (11-5) will likely need a better effort out of Roethlisberger next weekend against the AFC North champion Bengals (11-5) than what he provided against the Lions. He went 7 of 16 for 135 yards with two interceptions and a passer rating of 34.1 against the upset-minded Lions (5-11) at Heinz Field. He also ran for a touchdown.

His substandard play, however, could not undermine a Steelers team that needed to defeat the Lions in order to earn the AFC's sixth and final playoff berth.

The Steelers relied on special teams—Antwaan Randle El returned a punt 81 yards for the game's first score; Ricardo Colclough returned a kickoff 63 yards that led to the second—and the emotional lift provided by veteran tailback Jerome Bettis, who likely played his final game at Heinz Field, to overcome a 14-7 deficit.

Roethlisberger held himself accountable for this tougher-than-expected win.

"Lot of bad throws," he said. "Lot of them."

The Steelers had to wait 20 minutes after their win to discover who their first-round opponent would be. The Bengals, using a significant number of reserves, lost yesterday to the Kansas Chiefs and would have been the AFC's No. 4 seed if New England defeated Miami.

But the Patriots, also using a significant number of reserves, failed to convert a two-point conversion that

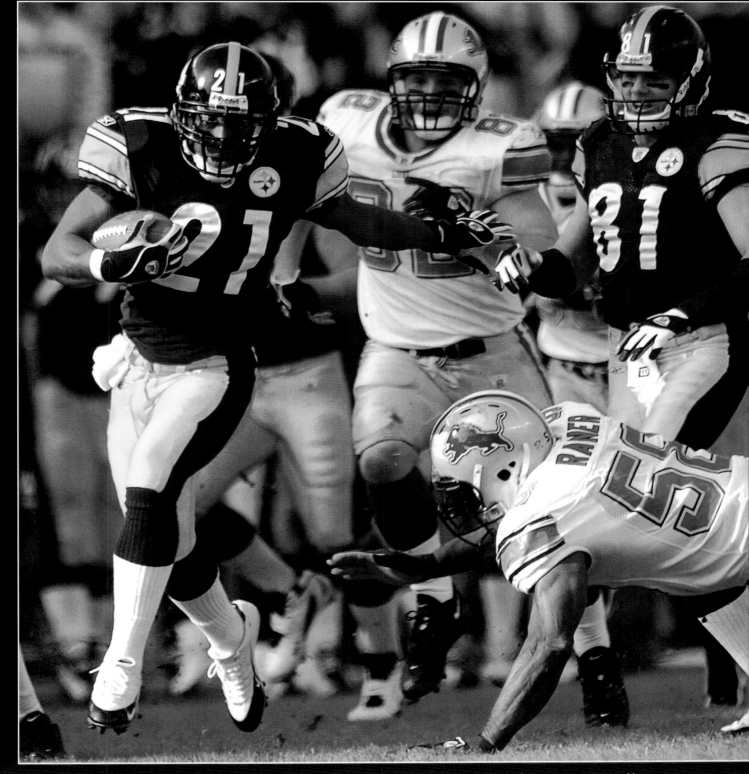

Pittsburgh cornerback Ricardo Colclough outpaces the Lions defense en route to a 63-yard kickoff return during the first quarter at Heinz Field. Jerome Bettis capped off the drive with the first of his three touchdowns. *Philip G. Pavely/Trib Total Media*

would have sent their game into overtime, giving the Bengals the No. 3 spot.

The conclusion of the Patriots-Dolphins game appeared on an overhead TV not far from where Steelers coach Bill Cowher was trying to hold his postgame news conference.

Cowher spoke briefly before waiting to get the final result of the New England game. Once he found out that the Patriots had lost, he discussed a Bengals team that went 1-1 against the Steelers this season, including a 27-13 loss in Week 6 at Paul Brown Stadium and a 38-31 victory in Week 12 at Heinz Field.

Turning the corner on Detroit's Shaun Rogers, Steelers quarterback Ben Roethlisberger runs for a 7-yard touchdown during the third quarter.
Christopher Horner/Trib Total Media

"There will be a lot of excitement in that stadium, their first playoff game in a long time (since 1990)," said Cowher. "It's a big, big challenge for us. We certainly have to play better than the last time we played them."

	1st	2nd	3rd	4th	Final
Lions	14	0	7	0	21
Steelers	14	7	14	0	35

SCORING SUMMARY

1st

PIT   A. Randle El 81-yard punt return (J. Reed kick).

DET   M. Pollard 11-yard pass from J. Harrington (J. Hanson kick)—8 plays, 59 yards in 4:00.

DET   C. Schlesinger 1-yard pass from J. Harrington (J. Hanson kick)—7 plays, 81 yards in 3:46.

PIT   J. Bettis 1-yard run (J. Reed kick)—6 plays, 33 yards in 3:12.

2nd

PIT   J. Bettis 5-yard run (J. Reed kick)—4 plays, 37 yards in 1:24.

3rd

PIT   J. Bettis 4-yard run (J. Reed kick)—7 plays, 77 yards in 4:00.

DET   R. Williams 15-yard pass from J. Harrington (J. Hanson kick)—12 plays, 63 yards in 5:28.

PIT   B. Roethlisberger 7-yard run (J. Reed kick)—8 plays, 82 yards in 4:50.

4th

No scoring.

TEAM STATS

	LIONS	STEELERS
1st Downs	16	20
3rd-Down Conversions	10-17	4-10
4th-Down Conversions	0-0	1-1
Punts-Average	6-39.2	4-41.0
Punts-Returns	2-1	2-79
Kickoffs-Returns	6-126	4-123
Int.-Returns	2-22	0-0
Penalties-Yards	5-47	2-15
Fumbles-Lost	3-2	0-0
Time Of Pos.	27:29	32:31
Total Net Yards	308	331
Total Plays	59	61
Net Yards Rushing	105	199
Rushes	25	44
Net Yards Passing	203	132
Comp.-Att.-Int.	17-33-0	7-16-2
Sacked-Yards Lost	1-9	1-3
Red Zone Efficiency	3-3-100%	4-4-100%

Ricardo Colclough (21) and James Farrior (51) tackle Detroit fullback Paul Smith during the second quarter.
Christopher Horner/Trib Total Media

"I'm going to go out to win football games and play as good as I can to help this team win. It came from a feeling like (I) lost it last year for the team, for making mistakes and not wanting to do it again and not wanting to make the same mistakes twice.

—QUARTERBACK BEN ROETHLISBERGER

55 JOEY PORTER

Motown met its match when the Steel City motor-mouth arrived in Detroit for Super Bowl XL. Steelers linebacker Joey Porter talks trash at virtually the same speed he plays football, with rapid-fire ferocity.

Difference is, he backs it up.

Don't believe it? Just meet him at the 50-yard line.

Always up for a confrontation and never one to back down from a verbal sparring session, Porter has proven to be as adept at shutting up his opponents as he is at slamming their quarterbacks down.

The three-time Pro Bowl selection had 10.5 sacks during the regular season, best among NFL linebackers, and recorded a sack in all three playoff games.

And his timing is impeccable.

Porter was in on two sacks of Peyton Manning in the Indianapolis Colts' next-to-last drive in the divisional playoff, and forced the Denver Broncos' Jake Plummer to fumble in the AFC Championship game.

"He wears his dad-gum heart on his sleeve, and he's a better football player when he plays that way," Steelers linebackers coach Keith Butler said. "Anybody who's ever watched him play knows that."

The seventh-year linebacker from Colorado State has been given free reign on free speech by Steelers coach Bill Cowher, despite an on-field ruckus that caused him to be ejected before a divisional game against Cleveland in 2004. Shortly thereafter, the NFL instituted a rule that players cannot cross their own 45-yard line in pregame warm-ups. Even so, that's a line Porter is willing to cross.

"He accepts me for who I am and he knows I play with a lot of emotion," Porter said of Cowher. "I'm going to go out there and do what I do best. He accepts

that, and he accepts how I play. As long as he appreciates what I do, he knows I'll feel the same way about him."

Porter isn't just the vocal leader of the Steelers defense, he's an inspirational character in their clubhouse. It was Porter who passed out Notre Dame throwback jerseys with Jerome Bettis' No. 6 to his teammates to wear for their arrival in Detroit, hometown of The Bus. And it was Porter who answered sharply to Seattle tight end Jerramy Stevens' comments that Bettis would leave "without that trophy."

After two days of toeing the company line – disappointing everyone at media day – Porter crossed it by ripping into Stevens and relishing his chance to back up the words.

Although the 6-foot-3, 250-pound Porter is a talented trash talker and feared pass-rusher, he's proven not to be bulletproof. Porter was shot in the backside outside a Colorado sports bar in September 2003, sending him a scare that could have threatened not only his career but his life. For a short time, Porter bit the bullet and tamed his trash-talking. But it didn't last.

"I know there are people out there who might not like him, how he comes off, but he's the kind of football player you want on your side," Steelers linebacker Clark Haggans said of Porter, a teammate at Colorado State. "The defense feeds off him the way the whole team feeds off coach (Bill) Cowher."

—Kevin Gorman

OPE'S OFFICIAL

BUNGLE IN THE JUNGLE

BY JOE BENDEL

Who Dey?

Dey the Bengals. And they found out what playoff football is about after a 15-year hiatus.

This oft-ridiculed franchise played well in the first half of this game with the Steelers at Paul Brown Stadium, despite losing Pro Bowl quarterback Carson Palmer, but ultimately succumbed to the Steelers' playoff experience.

The result was a 31-17 victory for the Steelers, who move on to the divisional round of the AFC playoffs against top-seed Indianapolis at the RCA Dome.

The Bengals, who won the AFC North Division championship, distributed a rap video this week featuring their signature refrain, "Who Dey?" Then, they did more rapping yesterday, accusing defensive tackle Kimo von Oelhoffen of deliberately injuring Palmer's ACL on the Bengals' second offensive play.

The Steelers, who overcame deficits of 10-0 and 17-7 in the first half, were not amused.

"For them to make a rap video, that was disrespectful to us," said wideout Hines Ward, who caught a 5-yard touchdown pass.

Linebacker Joey Porter said the Bengals spent too much time dwelling on Palmer's injury and not enough time riding the momentum they should have been building when they jumped to the early leads.

"When he got hurt, they were nervous," said Porter. "They were like, 'Oh, (shoot), we're going to lose without Carson.' Their coaches tried to jump on us, calling us chicken (droppings). So, they're sitting there dwelling on what happened to Carson and they lost focus on the bigger picture of trying to win the game."

The Steelers won a road playoff game for the first time in the 14-year Bill Cowher era. They are now 1-3.

They must win two more road playoff games to become the second team in NFL history to make it to the Super Bowl by traveling that route. The 1985 New England Patriots are the only team to accomplish the feat.

Quarterback Ben Roethlisberger went 14 of 19 for 208 yards with three touchdowns, no interceptions and a passer rating of 148.7, a near-perfect mark.

"It's experience," Cowher said. "He's been there."

The Bengals jumped to a 3-0 first-quarter lead at the game's outset. Palmer completed a 66-yard pass to rookie wideout Chris Henry. But the jubilation by the Bengals, however, ended when they discovered Palmer had gone down with a torn ACL after von Oelhoffen lightly wrapped up the knee—and bent it awkwardly—while crawling forward.

The Bengals drove to the Steelers' 5. But after a completion to T.J. Houshmandzadeh, Henry injured

Outside linebacker Clark Haggans brings down Cincinnati running back Rudi Johnson during the third quarter. *Christopher Horner/Trib Total Media*

his knee on the opposite side of the field. Kicker Shayne Graham's 23-yard field goal completed the drive.

The Steelers were forced to punt on their next possession and the Bengals offense, led by Kitna, drove 76 yards in seven plays, the final of which was a 20-yard touchdown run by Rudi Johnson to give the Bengals a 10-0 lead late in the first quarter.

The Steelers answered on their next drive, tying it, 10-7, on a perfectly executed screen pass to tailback Willie Parker, who let Bengals linebacker Brian Simmons get by him, then slipped to his right, where Roethlisberger got him the ball in the flat.

The Bengals scored on their third consecutive possession. This time, on a 7-yard touchdown pass to Houshmandzadeh, set up, in part, by an

Steelers quarterback Ben Roethlisberger scrambles to get away from the Bengals' defense during second-quarter action at Paul Brown Stadium.
Philip G. Pavely/Trib Total Media

Scoring untouched during the second quarter is Pittsburgh's Willie Parker. *Christopher Horner/Trib Total Media*

unsportsmanlike conduct call on Troy Polamalu that turned what would have been fourth-and-11 at the Steelers 17 into a first-and-goal at the 8. Polamalu threw a punch at Bengals center Rich Braham to draw the infraction.

The Steelers made it 17-14 on a 5-yard touchdown reception by Hines Ward, set up by a 54-yard catch by Wilson, and the once-confident Bengals slowly began questioning themselves.

"We stayed calm," Foote said, "they were nervous."

In the second half, things unraveled for the Bengals when they botched a field goal attempt that would have made it 20-14. The Steelers took over at

their own 34 and, after wideout Antwaan Randle El was interfered with near the goal line, Jerome Bettis sidestepped Bengals corner Tory James and gave the Steelers a lead, 21-17, they would never relinquish.

They pressured Kitna the rest of the way, scored two more times—including a trick-play in which Randle El took a direct snap, passed back to Roethlisberger, who hit a wide-open Cedrick Wilson for a 43-yard score—forced two interceptions and forged ahead in the postseason.

Antwaan Randle El can't handle a third-quarter pass, but Cincinnati's Kevin Kaesviham was called for pass interference on the play. The penalty set up a touchdown for the Steelers.
Philip G. Pavely/Trib Total Media

	1st	2nd	3rd	4th	Final
Steelers	0	14	14	3	31
Bengals	10	7	0	0	17

SCORING SUMMARY

1st
CIN S. Graham 23-yard FG—9 plays, 84 yards in 4:25.
CIN R. Johnson, 20-yard run (S. Graham kick)—7 plays, 76 yards in 3:26.

2nd
PIT W. Parker, 19-yard pass from B. Roethlisberger (J. Reed kick)—8 plays, 60 yards in 2:58.
CIN T. Houshmandzadeh, 7-yard pass from J. Kitna (S. Graham kick)—14 plays, 57 yards in 6:58.
PIT H. Ward, 5-yard pass from B. Roethlisberger (J. Reed kick)—6 plays, 76 yards in 2:25.

3rd
PIT J. Bettis, 5-yard run (J. Reed kick)—8 plays, 66 yards in 4:39.
PIT C. Wilson, 43-yard pass from B. Roethlisberger (J. Reed kick)—3 plays, 50 yards in 1:25.

4th
PIT J. Reed 21-yard FG—6 plays, 37 yards in 2:56.

TEAM STATS

	STEELERS	BENGALS
1st Downs	19	19
3rd-Down Conversions	6-11	9-16
4th-Down Conversions	0-0	0-1
Punts-Average	3-47.0	3-43.7
Punts-Returns	2-21	2-15
Kickoffs-Returns	4-94	6-127
Int-Returns	2-31	0-0
Penalties-Yards	6-39	7-90
Fumbles-Lost	0-0	2-0
Total Offense Plays-Yards	56-346	65-327
Rushes-Yards (Net)	34-144	20-84
Passing Yards (Net)	202	243
Comp-Att-Int	14-21-0	25-41-2
Sacked-Yards Lost	1-6	4-20
Red Zone Efficiency	3-5-60%	1-3-33%
Possession Time	28:57	31:03

Pittsburgh's Hines Ward (86) and Cedrick Wilson celebrate Wilson's third-quarter touchdown, a 43-yard pass from Ben Roethlisberger.
Philip G. Pavely/Trib Total Media

"When he got hurt, they were nervous. They were like, 'Oh, (shoot), we're going to lose without Carson.' Their coaches tried to jump on us, calling us chicken (droppings). So, they're sitting there dwelling on what happened to Carson and they lost focus on the bigger picture of trying to win the game."

—LINEBACKER JOEY PORTER

Cincinnati's Kevin Kaesviham is unable to stop Hines Ward from reeling in a second-quarter TD catch.
Philip G. Pavely/Trib Total Media

Steelers safety Troy Polamalu pulls Cincinnati's T.J. Houshmandzadeh to the ground during the third quarter of their AFC wildcard playoff at Paul Brown Stadium. *Christopher Horner/Trib Total Media*

Casey Hampton (98) and Larry Foote (50) force Bengals quarterback Jon Kitna to the turf during the third quarter. Kitna fumbled twice in the game. *Philip G. Pavely/Trib Total Media*

PORTER, STEELERS LASH OUT AFTER UPSET

BY JOE BENDEL

The Steelers have approached these NFL playoffs with an us-against-the-world mentality.

And the chip on their shoulders is getting larger by the victory.

"We play our best football (ticked) off," linebacker Joey Porter said. "And we're in a (ticked)-off mindset right now."

Several Steelers players, led by quarterback Ben Roethlisberger, chastised media members awaiting entrance into their locker room following this heart-pounding, 21-18 victory over the highly favored Indianapolis Colts in an AFC divisional game at the RCA Dome.

They entered as 9 1/2-point underdogs against the top-seeded Colts, who were coming off a bye.

"Y'all want to come in now?" Roethlisberger said, admonishing the media contingent just moments after the Steelers avoided a near-catastrophe when Colts kicker Mike Vanderjagt badly missed a 46-yard field goal that likely would have sent the game into overtime. "All the non-believers. You want to come in now?"

Roethlisberger was soft compared to what Porter said after this win, which earned the Steelers the distinction of being the first No. 6 seed in NFL history to reach a conference final.

They'll face the second-seeded Denver Broncos (14-3) at Invesco Field, with the winner moving on to Super Bowl XL in Detroit.

Porter accused the league of a conspiracy against the Steelers (13-5) after witnessing an interception by strong safety Troy Polamalu get reversed following video review. It seemed clear that Polamalu had possession of the ball on a diving catch—after which he rolled on the ground, then lost it while attempting to rise to his feet—but the officiating crew called the Colts offense back onto the field.

Four plays later, Indianapolis scored a touchdown and added a 2-point conversion to make the score 21-18 with 4:24 remaining. The Steelers ultimately survived, but only after Vanderjagt and the Colts failed to take advantage of Jerome Bettis' fumble at the Colts 2, which was returned to the 42 by Indianapolis defensive back Nick Harper with 1:01 to play.

"We dominated the whole game—till the referees wanted to help them," Porter said.

The outspoken linebacker, who challenged the Colts' toughness in the days leading up to the game, did not stop there.

Steelers strong safety Troy Polamalu recovers the ball after an apparent interception against the Colts during the fourth quarter. The play was later ruled an incomplete pass. *Philip G. Pavely/Trib Total Media*

Colts kicker Mike Vanderjagt walks dejectedly off the field after missing a potentially game-tying, 46-yard field goal with 21 seconds left.
Philip G. Pavely/Trib Total Media

"We play our best football (ticked) off—and we're in a (ticked)-off mindset right now."

—LINEBACKER JOEY PORTER

"I couldn't believe they were going to try to cheat us like that, for real," Porter said. "That was my thing. After we made that play (the near-interception), I thought the game was over. ... I'm going to get in trouble for it, I already know I'm going to get in trouble for it, but I'm ready to pay (the fine) anyway, because that's how mad I was with the refs out there. That was the worst I've ever been a part of. When you

Hines Ward and the Pittsburgh Steelers celebrate during the final seconds of a 21-18 victory over the Colts at the RCA Dome in Indianapolis.
Philip G. Pavely/Trib Total Media

play in games, you feel (sometimes) like it might not be going your way. But that was cheatin' right there, man."

Referee Pete Morelli had a different view of things.

"I had the defender catching the ball," Morelli said in a statement. "Before he got up, he hit it with his leg, with his other leg still on the ground. Therefore, he did not complete the catch."

Porter's response?

"C'mon, y'all seen it, man," he said. "What do we gotta do to make an interception? He caught the ball, rolled on the ground, got up and knocked the ball out of his hand with his knee. How can you say that's not an interception?

"It was just one of those games, the world wanted Indy to win so bad, they were going to do whatever they could. It was like the 9/11 year when they wanted the Patriots (who beat the Steelers in the AFC final) to win it for the world, just for the patriotic of the world. That's what they wanted for Indy today. They wanted (quarterback Peyton Manning) to win that game no matter what happened. They want him to win that game and they were going to give him all the opportunities to win it."

Winners of six in a row, the fired-up Steelers jumped on the Colts, riding the arm of Roethlisberger (14 of 24 for 197 yards with two touchdowns and an interception) en route to scoring on their first and third possessions for a 14-0 lead. Roethlisberger outplayed counterpart Manning (22 of 38 for 290 yards with a touchdown), considered by many to be the best in the game, with a passer rating of 95.3 to Manning's 90.9.

The Steelers stretched their advantage to 21-3 on a 1-yard scoring run by Bettis with 1:26 left in the third quarter before the Colts made it 21-10 on a 50-yard touchdown reception by tight end Dallas Clark with 14:09 to play.

The Colts added a 3-yard score by tailback Edgerrin James after the controversial call against Polamalu.

"It doesn't matter what I think," Polamalu said when asked about the call.

	1st	2nd	3rd	4th	Final
Steelers	14	0	7	0	21
Colts	0	3	0	15	18

SCORING SUMMARY

1st

PIT   A. Randle El, 6-yard pass from B. Roethlisberger (J. Reed kick)—10 plays, 84 yards in 5:35.

PIT   H. Miller, 7-yard pass from B. Roethlisberger (J. Reed kick)—7 plays, 72 yards in 2:53.

2nd

IND   M. Vanderjagt 20-yard FG—15 plays, 96 yards in 9:39.

3rd

PIT   J. Bettis, 1-yard run (J. Reed kick)—6 plays, 30 yards in 3:21.

4th

IND   D. Clark, 50-yard pass from P. Manning (M. Vanderjagt kick)—6 plays, 72 yards in 2:17.

IND   E. James, 3-yard run (P. Manning pass to R. Wayne)—6 plays, 80 yards in 1:39.

TEAM STATS

	STEELERS	COLTS
1st Downs	21	15
3rd-Down Conversions	6-14	3-13
4th-Down Conversions	2-2	1-2
Punts-Average	5-41.6	6-45.3
Punts-Returns	5-50	2—2
Kickoffs-Returns	3-55	3-52
Int-Returns	0-0	1-5
Penalties-Yards	2-8	9-67
Fumbles-Lost	1-1	1-0
Total Offense Plays-Yards	68-295	57-305
Rushes-Yards (Net)	42-112	14-58
Passing Yards (Net)	183	247
Comp-Att-Int	14-24-1	22-38-0
Sacked-Yards Lost	2-14	5-43
Red Zone Efficiency	3-4-75%	1-2-50%
Possession Time	34:52	25:08

"On the sports shows this week, people weren't even breaking down our game," linebacker Larry Foote said. "They were just going right to the other games, saying Indianapolis was going to beat Pittsburgh. But that doesn't matter. When the whistle blows, all that stuff is out the window."

The Steelers' Kimo von Oelhoffen (67) celebrates over the Colts' Jake Scott after Mike Vanderjagt's field goal went wide in the final minute of their playoff game. *Christopher Horner/Trib Total Media*

Indy's Mike Doss can't catch Steelers tight end Heath Miller as he snags a 36-yard pass from Ben Roethlisberger.
Christopher Horner/Trib Total Media

"Y'all want to come in now? ... All the non-believers—you want to come in now?"

—QUARTERBACK BEN ROETHLISBERGER

Linebacker Joey Porter, of the Pittsburgh Steelers, celebrates a second-quarter sack of Colts quarterback Peyton Manning.
Philip G. Pavely/Trib Total Media

Steelers receiver Antwaan Randle El hauls in a 13-yard pass in front of the Colts' Nick Harper during the third quarter of their AFC playoff game.
Christopher Horner/Trib Total Media

HEAD COACH BILL COWHER

Bill Cowher has a face made for NFL Films, which loves to capture the displeasure of the Steelers coach on the sidelines with his iron jaw jutting out.

Perhaps it was constructed for a specific purpose, as only such a steel-reinforced structure could contain Cowher's innards when he is spewing invective and spraying spittle, ready to take a swipe at an opposing player.

"Everyone thinks he's tough—he is—but he's a players' coach," Steelers receiver Hines Ward said. "His door is always open if you have a problem, or just want to talk. Yes, he gets angry, but most of the time, he's right."

Which is why Cowher is Teflon to the head coaching ranks, surviving an NFL-best 14 seasons and rewarding the Steelers' loyalty with a long-awaited Super Bowl title.

He did it the hard way, wearing white and winning on the road in the playoffs for the first time in a career that now warrants serious Hall of Fame consideration. Consider: Cowher has 153 career wins, second in Steelers history only to Chuck Noll and 15th all-time; has won eight division titles; has played in eight AFC Championship games and two Super Bowls. And he's only 48.

Before this Super season, Cowher was subject to scrutiny. Although, at 38, he became the youngest coach to reach a Super Bowl, the Steelers lost to the Dallas Cowboys in 1995. And Cowher was 1-4 in the AFC Championship game, all at either Three Rivers Stadium or Heinz Field. Prior to this season, he was 0-3 in road playoff games, a bad omen for a Steelers team that had to win its final four regular-season games just to qualify as a No. 6 seed.

The Steelers then beat, in order, the No. 3 seed, Cincinnati, No. 1 seed Indianapolis and No. 2 seed Denver on their home turf to reach Super Bowl XL.

Cowher is appreciative to the Rooneys that he's endured this long, especially with the NFL coaching carousel spinning dangerously out of control year after year. The Rooneys could have claimed just cause to fire Cowher after 6-10 and 7-9 seasons in the late 1990s, but resisted.

"Certainly, in some other places, a change may have been made," Cowher said. "I think we have a very healthy organization that starts at the top. There are no egos and we try to get things done as a team. Obviously, we're in a performance-now business and I don't think you take anything for granted, and I've never done that, so I'm not naive to think that if we don't have a bad year that I'll be another one of those guys that shows up on Black Monday.

"I think that's what keeps you going, is understanding that you are in a performance-now business, that you don't sit here and live off of your laurels and start reflecting too much or else someone else is going to pass you up. You have to stay a step ahead."

Cowher has always been two steps ahead. The Steelers hired the Crafton native, a 1975 graduate of Carlynton High School, to replace Noll on Jan. 21, 1992. Cowher was only 34, then the youngest coach in the league.

He had no ties to the Steelers organization, having played at North Carolina State before spending five years in the NFL as a special teams star and backup linebacker and seven as an assistant to Marty Schottenheimer.

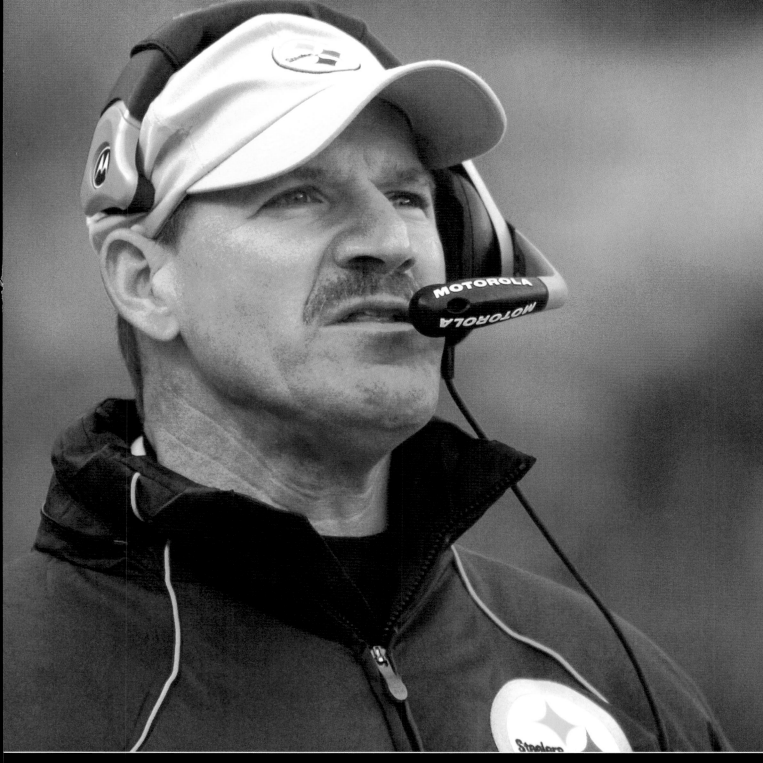

"I could see in him a guy who would have success over the long haul," Steelers chairman Dan Rooney said. "And that's what he's been. His roots have helped him. He's not one of those people who come to Pittsburgh and look around and think he's in some provincial town. He knows Pittsburgh, he understands the people, and he thinks of it as home. It's great to have him."

—Kevin Gorman

FAR FROM SATISFIED

BY JOE BENDEL

Go ahead and celebrate this Super victory all you want. Steelers chairman Dan Rooney is expecting more out of his storied franchise when it arrives in Detroit for Super Bowl XL.

"We're going to win the game," Rooney said in the jubilant Steelers' locker room Sunday, moments after his team defeated the Denver Broncos, 34-17, in the AFC Championship game at Invesco Field. "We're not going out there just saying, 'We're happy.' We're going to win. And every one of these guys feels that way."

Was Rooney being Joe Namath-esque with his forecast?

"I'm not making any predictions," he said. "I'm just saying what we're doing."

Who can argue? The Steelers are riding the arm of the league's hottest quarterback in Ben Roethlisberger and riding a never-before-seen magic carpet ride that has enabled them to make history by becoming the first No. 6 seed to advance to the Super Bowl.

By winning their third consecutive road playoff game—and beating the top three seeds in the AFC along the way—the Steelers earned a spot in Super Bowl XL against the top-seeded team from the NFC, the Seattle Seahawks, on Feruary 5 in Motown.

"We've been knocking on this door for years," cornerback Deshea Townsend said, pointing out that the Steelers had lost their previous three AFC finals in 1997, 2001 and 2004, all at home. "We decided that it was time to quit knocking. We came here and just kicked it in."

Running back Jerome Bettis fulfilled a season-long wish of potentially playing the final game of his career in his hometown of Detroit thanks to a Steelers team that jumped to a 24-3 halftime lead and easily dismantled the second-seeded Broncos.

It is the Steelers' first appearance in Super Bowl in 10 years. They lost to the Dallas Cowboys, 27-17, in Super Bowl XXX in Tempe, Ariz.

Bill Cowher, coaching his first AFC Championship game away from Pittsburgh, improved to 2-4 in the AFC final, and now has a chance to lead the Steelers to their first Super Bowl victory since 1980, when they won four in a span of six years.

"I have never had any doubts in my mind about him," team president Art Rooney II said of Cowher, who's been with the Steelers for 14 years, but has yet to win a Super Bowl. "That's for sure."

Added right guard Kendall Simmons, "Any other franchise probably would have found another coach because of all the years it's been since we've made the Super Bowl. But the Rooneys said, 'This man has what it takes. We know what he can do.' That's a testament to them. And it's a testament to coach Cowher."

After scoring a second-quarter touchdown against the Broncos, Steelers running back Jerome Bettis roars with the crowd.
Chaz Palla/Trib Total Media

The usually reserved Marvel Smith, the Steelers' left tackle, revealed a slight smile when he uttered the four most famous words in Pittsburgh.

"One for the thumb," he said. "One for the thumb—that's all I've heard since the first day I've been here. Now, we have a chance to seize the opportunity. We want to bring that championship back to Pittsburgh."

With the way the Steelers have been steamrolling the NFL over the past eight weeks—all victories— there is little reason to believe that a fifth Lombardi Trophy won't make its way back to the city.

Yesterday, Roethlisberger barely broke a sweat in slicing and dicing the Broncos, who were 9-0 at home this season and 11-0 dating back to 2004. The second-year quarterback, who struggled in the AFC final last season with three interceptions, finished 21 of 29 for 275 yards with two touchdowns, no interceptions and a passer rating of 124.9 yesterday.

He converted eight of his first 10 third-down conversions, manipulated Broncos rookie cornerback Domonique Foxworth and severely outplayed counterpart Jake Plummer, who accounted for all four of the Broncos' turnovers.

"Ben's playing Elway-like," Simmons said, referring to the only quarterback in Broncos history, John Elway, to lead the franchise to Super Bowl titles. "He has this quality that I'm going to get it done, regardless. He's a second-year guy, but it's like he's been around forever. He just sets the tone for everything."

Following guard Alan Faneca, quarterback Ben Roethlisberger scrambles for a first down during the second quarter.
Christopher Horner/Trib Total Media

Linebacker James Farrior rushes Denver quarterback Jake Plummer in the fourth quarter. *Chaz Palla/Trib Total Media*

Pittsburgh linebacker Larry Foote looks for running room after intercepting a pass from Jake Plummer in the fourth quarter.
Chaz Palla/Trib Total Media

Denver, which entered the game with the fewest turnovers in the NFL, could only look on as Plummer got rattled unmercifully. The quarterback's final fumble occurred with 4:52 remaining and the Broncos trailing, 27-17. Plummer dropped back to pass on fourth-and-10 at the Denver 20, but was sacked for the second time in as many plays by defensive end Brett Keisel, who also caused the turnover.

The Steelers took over at the Broncos' 17 and put the finishing touches on the win five plays later. Roethlisberger ran a bootleg left for a 4-yard touchdown that pushed the advantage to 34-17 with 2:59 remaining.

> ## "We're not going out there just saying, 'We're happy.' We're going to win. And every one of these guys feels that way."
>
> —STEELERS CHAIRMAN DAN ROONEY

The Steelers scored on all four of their first-half possessions. Kicker Jeff Reed hit a 47-yard field goal, Cedrick Wilson caught a 12-yard touchdown pass in the corner of the end zone, Bettis knifed in from 3 yards out and wideout Hines Ward caught a 17-yarder on a play in which Roethlisberger sidestepped the pass rush and fired the ball across his body deep into the end zone.

The Broncos attempted to make a game of it in the second half, closing the margin to 27-17 after a touchdown reception by Ashley Lelie and a 3-yard scoring run by Mike Anderson, but the turnover by Plummer sealed the loss.

Bettis capped things off by dumping Gatorade over the head of Cowher, who then firmly hugged Dan Rooney with less than two minutes to go.

"Mr. Rooney is a football guy," Cowher said. "He was very supportive during the three non-playoff years, and I'm very appreciative of that, and will always understand that and appreciate that patience. There's nothing greater, and nothing drives me more than to hopefully be able to hand him the first trophy. Nothing would make me more satisfied than to be able to do that."

	1st	2nd	3rd	4th	Final
Steelers	3	21	0	10	34
Broncos	0	3	7	7	17

SCORING SUMMARY

1st
PIT   J. Reed 47-yard FG—12 plays, 62 yards in 6:29.

2nd
PIT   C. Wilson, 12-yard pass from B. Roethlisberger (J. Reed kick)—5 plays, 39 yards in 2:53.
DEN   J. Elam 23-yard FG—12 plays, 55 yards in 5:31.
PIT   J. Bettis, 3-yard run (J. Reed kick)—14 plays, 80 yards in 7:28.
PIT   H. Ward, 17-yard pass from B. Roethlisberger (J. Reed kick)—4 plays, 38 yards in 1:41.

3rd
DEN   A. Lelie, 30-yard pass from J. Plummer (J. Elam kick)—5 plays, 80 yards in 2:24.

4th
PIT   J. Reed 42-yard FG—8 plays, 47 yards in 4:58.
DEN   M. Anderson, 3-yard run (J. Elam kick)—7 plays, 85 yards in 3:47.
PIT   B. Roethlisberger, 4-yard run (J. Reed kick)—5 plays, 17 yards in 1:53.

TEAM STATS

	STEELERS	BRONCOS
1st Downs	20	16
3rd-Down Conversions	10-16	5-11
4th-Down Conversions	0-0	2-3
Punts-Average	4-37.0	2-43.5
Punts-Returns	1-13	0-0
Kickoffs-Returns	2-42	5-121
Int-Returns	2-15	0-0
Penalties-Yards	8-61	4-20
Fumbles-Lost	1-0	2-2
Total Offense Plays-Yards	64-358	54-308
Rushes-Yards (Net)	33-90	21-97
Passing Yards (Net)	268	211
Comp-Att-Int	21-29-0	18-30-2
Sacked-Yards Lost	2-7	3-12
Red Zone Efficiency	4-5-80%	1-2-50%
Possession Time	36:07	23:53

Head coach Bill Cowher gets a Gatorade shower from Jerome Bettis in the final minute of play against the Broncos in Denver.
Philip G. Pavely/Trib Total Media

"We've been knocking on this door for years. We decided that it was time to quit knocking. We came here and just kicked it in."

—CORNERBACK DESHEA TOWNSEND

Steelers quarterback Ben Roethlisberger holds the AFC Championship trophy with team owners Art (left) and Dan Rooney after the Steelers beat the Broncos 34-17. *Chaz Palla/Trib Total Media*

Steelers running back Willie Parker flies down field for a 75-yard touchdown just after the start of the second half. The TD was a Super Bowl record. *Barry Reeger/Trib Total Media*

SUPER STEELERS

BY JOE BENDEL

These Super Steelers out-rocked the Rolling Stones, out-socked the Seattle Seahawks and walked out of this Terrible Towel-covered city with that long-awaited "One for the Thumb."

Yes, Pittsburgh, your Steelers are Super Bowl champions. Again.

For the fifth time.

This emotionally charged, 21-10 victory over the Seahawks on Sunday at Ford Field elicited tears from tough-guy coach Bill Cowher, who waited 14 years for an NFL championship and brought the Lombardi Trophy back to the Rooney family after a 26-year drought.

In the magical moments after the game, Super Bowl MVP Hines Ward and retiring running back Jerome Bettis choked back tears while chairman Dan Rooney accepted the illuminating hardware from NFL commissioner Paul Tagliabue.

"How does it feel to have the trophy back in the Steel City?" Tagliabue said, confetti fluttering all around.

Humble as always, Rooney deflected any credit directed toward him.

"It's wonderful. I could say that's where (the trophy) belongs, but it belongs to these wonderful players and coach Bill Cowher and his staff," Rooney said.

Cowher, flanked by his wife, Kaye, and standing at a podium adjacent to his three daughters, shook his head in mocking disapproval.

"Mr. Rooney," the veteran coach said, beaming, "I've been waiting a long time to do this. This is yours, man."

The 73-year-old patriarch of one of the NFL's model franchises then held the trophy above his head and celebrated this Super Bowl XL title, which put the Steelers in the elite company of the Dallas Cowboys and San Francisco 49ers as five-time Super Bowl champions.

And the thing that will distinguish this edition of the Steelers is the path they took to reach the summit of the NFL mountain. They became the first team in league history to enter the postseason as the No. 6 seed and to win three road playoff games en route to the Super Bowl title.

They embraced their role as underdogs—even though they were favored to defeat the Seahawks—and they followed the lead of their fiery, 48-year-old coach, a native of Crafton, who fulfilled a lifelong dream by leading his hometown team to an NFL title.

As the final seconds ticked away, Cowher laughed and embraced his players on the sideline. He thrust his arms high in the air after being doused with Gatorade. And he cried. ...

Steelers linebacker Larry Foote celebrates after bringing down Shaun Alexander. The Pittsburgh defense was able to contain Alexander and did not allow him to score in the game. *Christopher Horner/Trib Total Media*

Steelers cornerback Deshea Townsend celebrates after sacking Seahawks quarterback Matt Hasselbeck in the fourth quarter. Hasselbeck was sacked three times in the game. *Chaz Palla/Trib Total Media*

And he cried.

This was a moment of relief for a man who's been accused of not being able to "win the big game," after going 1-4 in AFC finals and 0-1 in the Super Bowl (in 1995) before this unforgettable season. It was also a moment of pure, heart-tugging emotion, as he sought out his wife and daughters and firmly put his arms around them.

No longer will Cowher have to deal with comparisons to his predecessor, Chuck Noll, who won four Super Bowls in a six-year span during the 1970s.

And his players will no longer have to deal with the seemingly never-ending discussions about the Steelers' teams that were led by Terry Bradshaw, Franco Harris and "Mean" Joe Greene.

Cowher has his own identity now, one that involves the words "world champion."

And his players have their own identity now, as they too will be labeled "world champions" for life.

"It's almost surreal," Cowher said, as he accepted the Lombardi Trophy in front of an estimated 50,000 Steelers fans. "This is a special group of coaches, a special group of players. I was one small part of this, trust me. These guys were so resilient. ... It starts at the top. I can't be more happy for Mr. Rooney, for the players, for the coaches and for the city of Pittsburgh.

"We are proud. Now, we've got our own little niche right now. We're taking this baby back home. And we're going to enjoy it."

Quarterback Ben Roethlisberger sends the ball down field in the first quarter. Roethlisberger completed nine of 21 passes en route to beating the Seahawks 21-10 in Detroit. *Chaz Palla/Trib Total Media*

"I came back to win a championship—mission accomplished.
With that, I have to bid farewell."

—RUNNING BACK JEROME BETTIS

Detroit native Jerome Bettis has room to run against the Seahawks. Bettis ran for 43 yards; his longest was a 12-yard run.
Chaz Palla/Trib Total Media

Players such as Ben Roethlisberger, who became the youngest quarterback in NFL history to win a Super Bowl, surely will savor this win. As will wideout Ward, who put his name beside former Steelers Super Bowl MVPs Bradshaw, Harris, and Lynn Swann.

Meanwhile, Bettis got to close out his 13-year career on a cloud, winning the Super Bowl in his hometown of Detroit.

"I came back to win a championship—mission accomplished," Bettis said. "With that, I have to bid farewell."

At halftime of yesterday's game, Rolling Stones lead man Mick Jagger belted out, "I can't get no satisfaction," an anthem that could have served as the theme for Steelers' fans the past 26 years.

But when the game ended, those same fans, who filled a significant portion of Ford Field, got to witness this franchise's return to glory on the biggest stage in sports.

Yes, they finally got their satisfaction.

"This was definitely a home game for us," said safety Chris Hope, who was asked what he thought it would be like back in Pittsburgh after this Super win. "That's if there's a city there. The city might go under siege."

	1st	2nd	3rd	4th	Final
Steelers	0	7	7	7	21
Seahawks	3	0	7	0	10

SCORING SUMMARY

1st
SEA   J.Brown 47-yard FG—7 plays, 22 yards in 3:39.

2nd
PIT   B.Roethlisberger 1-yard run (J.Reed kick)—11 plays, 59 yards in 6:20.

3rd
PIT   W.Parker 75-yard run (J.Reed kick)—2 plays, 75 yards in 0:22.

SEA   J.Stevens 16-yard pass from M.Hasselbeck (J.Brown kick)—3 plays, 20 yards in 0:53.

4th
PIT   H.Ward 43-yard pass from A.Randle El (J.Reed kick)—4 plays, 56 yards in 1:50.

TEAM STATS

	SEAHAWKS	STEELERS
1st Downs	20	14
3rd-Down Conversions	5-17	8-15
4th-Down Conversions	1-2	0-0
Punts-Average	6-50.2	6-48.7
Punts-Returns	4-71	2-43
Kickoffs-Returns	5-128	4-79
Int.-Returns	2-76	1-24
Penalties-Yards	7-70	3-20
Fumbles-Lost	0-0	0-0
Time Of Pos.	33:02	26:58
Total Net Yards	396	339
Total Plays	77	56
Net Yards Rushing	137	181
Rushes	25	33
Net Yards Passing	259	158
Comp.-Att.	26-49	10-22
Yards Per Pass	5.0	6.9
Sacked-Yards Lost	1-8	3-14
Red Zone Efficiency	1-3-33%	1-2-50%

Elizabeth Stanton, of Homewood-Brushton, along with thousands of other fans, cheer on the Steelers downtown during a Victory Rally on February 2, 2006. *Keith Hodan/Trib Total Media*

After diving from the 1-yard line, Ben Roethlisberger looks for a ruling on his touchdown. The play was reviewed, but the ruling on the field was upheld. *Philip G. Pavely/Trib Total Media*

"Mr. Rooney, I've been waiting a long time to do this. This is yours, man."

—HEAD COACH BILL COWHER TO STEELERS CHAIRMAN DAN ROONEY

Seattle kicker Josh Brown misses a field goal attempt. Brown missed two field goals against the Steelers.
Barry Reeger/Trib Total Media

BETTIS CLOSES WITH STORYBOOK ENDING

BY KEVIN SMITH

Jerome Bettis wanted to roll out of the NFL with a Super Bowl title in his hometown of Detroit.

On February 5, 2006, he got his wish, as the Steelers gave him a championship send-off with a 21-10 victory in Super Bowl XL at Ford Field.

Bettis announced his retirement from the NFL after the game and finishes as the league's fifth-leading rusher with 13,662 regular-season yards and 91 touchdowns.

Padding those numbers didn't mean anything to Bettis this season.

He had one number in mind, and that was 40, as in Super Bowl XL.

"I came back to win a championship," Bettis said. "Mission accomplished. With that, I have to bid farewell."

In the closing seconds of last year's AFC Championship game, a tearful Ben Roethlisberger promised Bettis a shot at a title if he came back this season.

"It was awesome," Roethlisberger said. "I promised Jerome last year that I would get him here—I didn't promise I would win it, but I promised I would get him here.

"Then, after the Cincinnati game, I promised him that I would get him four game balls. I'm just glad I could fulfill the promises that I made to him."

The setting for that farewell could not have been better in a movie script.

"This is a storybook for him," Steelers linebacker Clark Haggans said. "That is all I can really say. This is a storybook for him."

Christopher Horner/Trib Total Media

"It's truly an exclamation point to his career.
He's one of the all-time NFL greats and a true icon."

— STEELERS TACKLE MAX STARKS

Bettis didn't finish with a touchdown in his final game, but he rushed for 43 yards on 14 carries.

He was instrumental in the fourth quarter, carrying seven times on the Steelers' final possession while they ate nearly five minutes off the clock.

"It's amazing, truly amazing," Bettis said. "I am truly the happiest player on this field. I'm the happiest player in the world.

"We are the champions of the world. They can't take that from us. It's all over. There aren't any games left. It's an unbelievable moment."

It's a moment that didn't seem possible when the Steelers dropped to 7-5 after a 38-31 home loss to Cincinnati.

But Steelers rallied to win their last eight games, and Bettis became one of the team's rallying points.

"My team put me on their backs, and they didn't let me down," Bettis said. "These guys were tremendous. They brought it home for us."

Bettis was the main figure of the two weeks leading up to Super Bowl XL.

He sat like a king Tuesday during Media Day, perched in a booth with the hoard of media surrounding him.

He sponsored a charity bowling tournament Thursday, received a key to the city, had his jersey retired by his high school and had his mother cook dinner for more than 40 of his teammates.

"It's truly an exclamation point to his career," Steelers tackle Max Starks said. "He's one of the all-time NFL greats and a true icon.

"It is truly an honor to have played with him the two years that I have been here and to finally give him the opportunity to hold that Vince Lombardi Trophy up in the air in his hometown."

When the Steelers were announced before the game, the players sent Bettis out alone. He raced from the tunnel and did a little dance at the middle of the field.

"It was Jerome (Bettis) day today," Steelers linebacker Joey Porter said.

And the setting could not have been more perfect.

"You know what? I had so many people come out on to the field, and they were tearing up. And to hear the ovation of the crowd and to hear the people I grew up cheering for me in the Super Bowl, it was incredible," Bettis said. "It's better than I ever thought it would be."

86 HINES WARD
SUPER BOWL MVP

Prior to the start of this super season, Hines Ward held out for a new contract.

After waiting a bit longer than Ward would have preferred, the Steelers rewarded him with the richest contract in franchise history.

In Super Bowl XL, Ward made sure that every dime the Rooney family spent on him was worth five times its weight in silver.

Ward caught five passes for 123 yards and a key fourth-quarter touchdown (from fellow wideout Antwaan Randle El, no less) as the Steelers won their first Super Bowl championship in 26 seasons—and NFL record-tying fifth overall—with a hard-fought 21-10 victory against the Seattle Seahawks.

For his spectacular efforts, Ward, who also rushed once for 18 yards, was named the game's most valuable player.

"It's been a wild ride—from the contract negotiation to winning the Super Bowl MVP. I'm at a loss of words," Ward said, shortly after being handed the keys to a 2007 black Cadillac Escalade. "I've always tried to prove the naysayers wrong, and this time, I really did."

Ward becomes the second wide receiver in Steelers' history to win the Super Bowl MVP.

Hall-of-Famer Lynn Swann won the award for his spectacular four-catch, 161-yard performance in Super Bowl X against the Dallas Cowboys.

"If you look at the history of the Pittsburgh Steelers, people talk about (Lynn) Swann and (John) Stallworth making spectacular plays in the Super Bowl," Ward said. "I never felt I belonged with those guys. Now, I do."

Ward has long since eclipsed most of Swann's receiving yards and is second to only Stallworth in total receiving yards and touchdown catches. He's already the franchise's career receptions leader, having passed Stallworth midway through the regular season.

Last night, Ward was not as flashy as either Swann in Super Bowl X or Stallworth in Super Bowl XIV.

But as Ward said, flash has never been a part of his game. Consistency has—not that Ward felt he was particularly consistent last night.

He dropped what should have been his first touchdown pass early in the game because he was too focused on the positioning of his feet and acknowledged that he left a lot of plays on the field against the Seahawks.

Anybody who has followed his career knows that leaving anything on the field is not Ward's style.

But he made the plays that mattered—a 37-yard second-quarter catch that set up the Steelers for their first touchdown and the 43-yard touchdown reception from Randle El that essentially sealed Super Bowl XL.

"After that play, it began to sink in that we might win this thing. ... I think that really clinched it for us," Ward said of his touchdown reception—the eighth, and no doubt most monumental, of his postseason career.

Swann was in attendance last night to watch Ward, a third-round pick out of Georgia in 1998, prove his doubters wrong.

Much of the focus prior to Super Bowl XL fell upon Steelers quarterback Ben Roethlisberger and retiring running back Jerome Bettis.

Ward, as he has been most of his under-the-radar-but-storied Steelers career, was seemingly an afterthought.

He won't be anymore.

Ward wept almost uncontrollably after the Steelers were defeated in the AFC Championship game last season—crying because he thought that loss had signified the end of Jerome Bettis' career and, thus, a wasted opportunity to get Bettis a long-coveted championship.

Last night, Ward delivered Bettis that title.

"I'm an emotional guy, but I promised Jerome I wouldn't cry," Ward said, as he flashed his trademark wide grin. "This is pretty good, though."

Ward, whose string of four consecutive Pro Bowls came to an end this season, entered Super Bowl XL with 10 receptions for 137 yards and two touchdowns in three postseason games—not exactly the kind of numbers that foreshadowed a Super Bowl MVP performance.

But Ward has always taken great pride in proving skeptics wrong, and he did so against Seattle.

"People kept saying things all year—that this guy can't get it done," Ward said of the critics who argued he couldn't produce at a high level without Plaxico Burress, who left the Steelers during the offseason to sign with the New York Giants. "You just have to go out and prove those people wrong.

Christopher Horner/Trib Total Media

"Here I (was) playing in the Super Bowl. And for me to have my name mentioned with some of the MVPs that played in the Super Bowl ... words can't describe it.

"It's totally a dream come true."

PASSING

PASSING	Yds	Yds/Att	Yds/Gm	Att	Comp	Comp %	TD	INT	Sacked	Rating
Ben Roethlisberger	2250	8.9	150.0	252	161	63.9	17	7	22	103.4
Tommy Maddox	406	5.7	27.1	71	34	47.9	2	4	8	51.7
Charlie Batch	246	6.8	16.4	36	23	63.9	1	1	1	81.5

RUSHING

RUSHING	Yds	Att	Yds/Att	Yds/Gm	TD's	Fumb
Willie Parker	1067	229	4.7	71.1	4	0
Jerome Bettis	327	100	3.3	21.8	6	0
Verron Haynes	257	70	3.7	17.1	3	1
Duce Staley	148	38	3.9	9.9	1	0
Antwaan Randle El	72	11	6.5	4.8	0	3
Ben Roethlisberger	64	28	2.3	4.3	2	1
Charlie Batch	30	11	2.7	2.0	1	0
Tommy Maddox	26	8	3.3	1.7	0	2
Dan Kreider	21	3	7.0	1.4	0	0
Hines Ward	10	3	3.3	0.7	0	1
Noah Herron	2	3	0.7	0.1	0	0
Cedrick Wilson	0	1	0.0	0.0	0	0

RECEIVING

RECEIVING	Rec	Yds	Yds/Rec	Yds/Game	TD
Hines Ward	68	935	13.8	62.3	11
Heath Miller	36	397	11.0	26.5	6
Antwaan Randle El	34	545	16.0	36.3	1
Cedrick Wilson	26	451	17.3	30.1	0
Willie Parker	17	201	11.8	13.4	1
Verron Haynes	10	110	11.0	7.3	0
Quincy Morgan	9	150	16.7	10.0	2
Dan Kreider	7	43	6.1	2.9	0
Duce Staley	6	34	5.7	2.3	0
Jerome Bettis	4	40	10.0	2.7	0
Jerame Tuman	3	57	19.0	3.8	0
Matt Kranchick	1	6	6.0	0.4	0

SCORING

SCORING	Pts	TD	FG	XP	2-Pt	Sfty
Jeff Reed	112	0	24	40	0	0
Hines Ward	66	11	0	0	0	0
Heath Miller	36	6	0	0	0	0
Jerome Bettis	36	6	0	0	0	0
Willie Parker	30	5	0	0	0	0
Verron Haynes	18	3	0	0	0	0
Antwaan Randle El	12	2	0	0	0	0
Ben Roethlisberger	12	2	0	0	0	0
Quincy Morgan	12	2	0	0	0	0
Charlie Batch	6	1	0	0	0	0
Duce Staley	6	1	0	0	0	0
Troy Polamalu	6	1	0	0	0	0
Larry Foote	2	0	0	0	0	1

KICKING

KICKING	FGM	FGA	Acc(%)	XPM	XPA	Pts
Jeff Reed	24	29	82	37	37	109

PUNTING

PUNTING	Avg	Punts	Yds
Chris Gardocki	41.9	63	2639
Ben Roethlisberger	36.0	2	72

DEFENSE

DEFENSE	Tackles	Assists	Sacks	INT	Fum Rec	Sfty	TD
James Farrior	112	43	1.0	0	1	0	0
Larry Foote	98	23	3.0	0	1	1	0
Chris Hope	90	24	0.0	3	1	0	0
Ike Taylor	81	14	0.0	1	2	0	0
Troy Polamalu	81	16	3.0	2	2	0	1
Clark Haggans	58	17	9.0	0	0	0	0
Joey Porter	55	17	11.0	2	1	0	0
Deshea Townsend	50	11	3.0	2	1	0	0
Casey Hampton	40	16	0.0	0	0	0	0
Aaron Smith	34	7	2.0	1	0	0	0
Kimo Von Oelhoffen	32	10	3.0	0	0	0	0
James Harrison	31	6	3.0	1	0	0	0
Brett Keisel	17	5	3.0	0	0	0	0
Bryant McFadden	16	0	1.0	1	1	0	0
Clint Kriewaldt	16	3	0.0	0	0	0	0
Mike Logan	15	4	0.0	0	0	0	0
Ricardo Colclough	13	2	1.0	1	0	0	0
Travis Kirschke	12	6	1.0	0	1	0	0
Tyrone Carter	11	2	1.0	1	2	0	0
Willie Williams	10	3	0.0	0	0	0	0
Chris Hoke	6	3	0.0	0	0	0	0
Andre Frazier	2	0	0.0	0	0	0	0

KICK RETURNS

KICK RETURNS	Avg	Ret	Yds	TD
Quincy Morgan	26.2	20	523	0
Ike Taylor	19.7	3	59	0
Ricardo Colclough	19.5	21	410	0
Cedrick Wilson	17.7	3	53	0
Antwaan Randle El	16.0	1	16	0
Brett Keisel	11.5	2	23	0
Dan Kreider	3.0	1	3	0

PUNT RETURNS

PUNT RETURNS	Avg	Ret	Yds	TD
Ike Taylor	19.0	1	19	0
Antwaan Randle El	8.8	42	369	1
Chidi Iwuoma	3.0	1	3	0

TIGHT ENDS

TIGHT ENDS	Rec	Yds	Avg	Avg/Gm	TD
Heath Miller	36	397	11.0	26.5	6
Jerame Tuman	3	57	19.0	3.8	0
Matt Kranchick	1	6	6.0	0.4	0

Steelers Head Coach Bill Cowher gets an ice bath from his players in the final seconds of Super Bowl XL. *Barry Reeger/Trib Total Media*

On a pass from Steelers wide receiver Antwaan Randle El, Hines Ward leaps into the end zone for a 43-yard touchdown in the fourth quarter of Super Bowl XL. *Chaz Palla/Trib Total Media*

ACKNOWLEDGMENTS

Columnists

Joe Starkey

Mike Prisuta

Reporters

Joe Bendel

Joe Rutter

Jim Rodenbush

Rick Starr

Rob Biertempfel

Rob Rossi

Kevin Gorman

Photographers

Chaz Palla

Christopher Horner

Philip G. Pavely

Joe Appel

Steven Adams

Barry Reeger

Keith Hodan

Deputy Managing Editor, Design

James M. Kubus

Executive Sports Editor

Kevin Smith

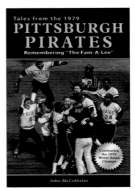
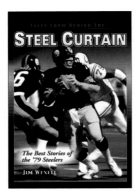
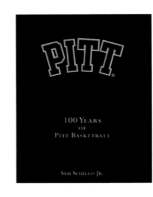
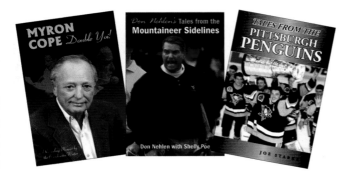